use your words

A WRITING GUIDE
FOR MOTHERS

BY KATE HOPPER

FOREWORD BY HOPE EDELMAN

VIVA
EDITIONS

Published in the United States by Viva Editions, an imprint of Cleis Press Inc., 2246 Sixth Street, Berkeley CA 94710.

Printed in the United States.
Cover design: Scott Idleman/Blink
Cover photograph: Phil Ashley/Getty Images
Text design: Frank Wiedemann
Author photograph: Nancy Reins

First Edition.
10 9 8 7 6 5 4 3 2 1

Trade paper ISBN: 978-1-936740-12-3
E-book ISBN: 978-1-936740-22-2

Library of Congress Cataloging-in-Publication Data

Hopper, Kathryn Ann, 1972-
    Use your words : a writing guide for mothers / by Kate Hopper. -- 1st ed.
        p. cm.
    Includes index.
    ISBN 978-1-936740-12-3 (pbk. : alk. paper)
    1. Creative writing. 2. Creative nonfiction. 3. Mothers--Authorship. 4. Motherhood.
    5. Parenting. I. Title.
    PN145.H65 2012
    808'.0420852--dc23
                        2012001067

Advance praise for *Use Your Words*

Kate Hopper's *Use Your Words* demonstrates how the universal experiences of motherhood can be transformative through storytelling, and offers practical, thoughtful, and insightful guidance to any writer interested in the process of translating life experience into story.

—Andrea Buchanan,
author of *The Daring Book for Girls, Mother Shock:
Loving Every (Other) Minute of It,* and six other books

Kate Hopper knows: how to inspire the budding writer to find her voice and her truth; what it takes to keep that writer going; and the words of advice and inspiration every writer needs to hear. In Hopper's assured, experienced hands, women and mothers will glean not only the all-important elements of craft, they will feel emboldened and prepared to take the essential steps from idea to finished piece. This is a beautiful, polished guide to craft and story-telling for writing about motherhood and beyond.

—Vicki Forman,
author of *This Lovely Life: A Memoir of Premature Motherhood*

The only reason I've ever wanted to visit Minnesota was for the chance to meet Kate Hopper and take one of her writing classes. Thankfully, Kate has translated her successful Use Your Words writing class onto paper and created a personal, practical guide for any mother writer. Grounding each lesson with terrific essays and poems by a wide variety of writers, Kate offers a solid education in creative writing plus a range of approachable assignments designed to make readers put the book down and start writing.

—Caroline Grant,
editor in chief of Literary Mama and co-editor of *Mama, PhD:
Women Write About Motherhood and Academic Life*

Part writing workshop, part anthology, part mothers' group between two covers, *Use Your Words* is so much more than an instruction manual. It is also a readable, powerful call to the page for every woman in the process of giving birth to herself as a writer. If you have ever wondered whether motherhood is a viable literary subject, or whether you have a mothering story worth telling, Kate Hopper's beautifully written book will answer that question once and for all—with compelling excerpts, exercises to inspire you, and clear, practical teachings on matters of voice, structure, and style.

—Katrina Kenison,
author of *The Gift of an Ordinary Day* and *Mitten Strings for God*

Kate Hopper has been a valuable part of our teaching staff since 2006 and has contributed to the success of the Loft Literary Center. Her students rave about her. She is accessible and friendly and always enthusiastic and supportive of them; she makes them feel that their writing is valuable and that their work is important work. One of her Loft students said, "I've taken many writing classes, and this class was the most supportive, helpful class I've ever had, while still giving extremely helpful critique." Another said, "I loved Kate as an instructor! She was so encouraging and supportive of everyone's efforts, but also very knowledgeable about the craft of writing, as well as prose revision. I would take another class from her in a minute."

—Brian Malloy,
Education Director of The Loft Literary Center

Finally a book to teach parents how to write! In readable, interesting, practical prose, *Use Your Words* gives moms what they need to know to write about their children's most precious moments. A tremendous resource for bloggers, teachers, lay and professional writers.

—Jennifer Margulis, PhD,
author of *Toddler: Real-Life Stories of Those Fickle, Irrational, Urgent, Tiny People We Love*

Use Your Words brings a unique voice to the world of writing guides: honest, forthright, funny. Reading it felt like sitting down for a writing tête-a-tête with a literary friend and practicing writer. Because her voice is real, Kate welcomes beginners with trustworthy invitations to reach deep, and speaks to the practicing writer with new levels of insight about writing motherhood literature. When a teacher/author takes a risk with voice and really bares herself, her students/readers can do no less than rise to the challenge. This book is original in covering the specific areas where the experience of motherhood fires, and complicates, the task of writing. Also, this book is funny! I thought I was reading it just for fun—I knew it would be fun—but the surprise for me was the spur in the ribs I got to write, and write well.

—Bonnie J. Rough,
author of *Carrier: Untangling the Danger in My DNA*

use your
words

To all the mothers who have generously shared their stories with me.
I thank you.

And to Stella and Zoë: Without you these words would not exist.
Thank you for making my life rich with your laughter and antics.

Writing—like living, like parenting, like any form of creation—is always an act of faith anyway, a struggle, a dare to somehow get onto a blank sheet of paper some approximation of experience in a single, unique voice.

—PENNY WOLFSON

TABLE OF CONTENTS

THE TRANSITION TO MOTHERHOOD, WHETHER by birth or adoption, is a universally defining event for women, setting a new tone for all that follows. The known world abruptly expands to include a love so fierce and so big a woman transforms under its spell. And with this profound shift inevitably comes an avalanche of new themes to explore, and stories to tell.

Literature has long celebrated images of the selfless, doting maternal figure and the crafty, conniving matriarch infused with her own power. Only in the past few decades have the voices of real mothers, from real families, emerged to describe, analyze, reflect on, and expose the triumphs and challenges of the job. From the humor columns of Erma Bombeck in the 1960s to the self-probing personal essays of Joyce Maynard and Anna Quindlen in the 1980s, Anne Lamott's groundbreaking 1993 memoir about her son's first year, *Operating Instructions,* and present-day memoirs by authors such as Beth Kephart, Ayun Halliday, and Rachel Cusk, mothers' stories find widespread, receptive audiences. Slowly, they're making the cultural migration from

"Parenting" and "Women's Issues" shelves to the gender-neutral "Essays," "Memoir," and "Biography," where they rightfully belong. For these are not "women's" stories being told; they are cultural stories, human stories, sharing details and reflections about the most fundamental family relationships and, in the process, revealing how our next generation is being raised.

Turning personal experience into readable prose is a daunting process for anyone, and carving out the time to do so isn't easy with a house full of short people in need of constant attention. In *Use Your Words*, Kate Hopper offers a practical and accessible road map for any mother who'd like to get started. Part instructor, part motivator, part best friend, Kate guides mother-writers from idea through finished product, offering encouragement and hard-earned wisdom along the way. She intersperses poems, essays, and short memoirs by known writers such as Cecelie S. Berry, Judith Ortiz Cofer, and Chitra Divakaruni—and emerging writers from The Loft Literary Center in Minneapolis—with passages about the craft of writing, and ends each chapter with helpful short exercises for readers to try at home. Any mother who picks it up and follows the carefully planned instructions will be able to call herself a mother-writer by the final page.

It's rare for a book about writing to strike such a perfect balance between instruction and example, while offering inspiration and practical advice at the same time. But then we mothers are pros at multitasking. So while the kids are sleeping, off at school, or otherwise occupied, open your laptop. Pick up your pen. Your stories are waiting to be told.

Hope Edelman
Author of the international bestseller *The Possibility of Everything*

༄ ༅ ༆

WHY *USE YOUR WORDS?*

WHEN I WAS SEVEN MONTHS PREGNANT WITH MY first daughter, Stella, and just beginning the third year of the MFA program in creative writing at the University of Minnesota, I became suddenly and severely ill with preeclampsia, a disease that affects 5–8 percent of all pregnancies and is responsible for over 77,000 maternal deaths worldwide every year. My daughter was born via C-section almost eight weeks early, and she spent four weeks in the neonatal intensive care unit (NICU). While she was hospitalized, growing and learning to breathe and eat, she went into respiratory distress, developed jaundice, anemia, a bowel obstruction, a Grade 1 intraventricular hemorrhage, and sepsis, a systemic blood infection which occurred when the IV line in her arm pulled loose from its vein and filled her tiny shoulder with fluid. She recovered from each of these, and after a month, when she still weighed less than four and a half pounds, we took her home. But because of her immature immune system and the fact that it was cold-and-flu season in Minnesota, we couldn't take her out in public. I withdrew from graduate school and spent five long months inside with my fragile daughter: I walked my fussy infant around our dining room table for hours and hours each day; I attempted, unsuccessfully, to nurse her; I passed the weeks in an exhausted daze, unable to get my mind around the ways my life had changed. And for the first time in my life, I felt desperate for words, for some way to express the changes I was undergoing as an isolated new mother.

Stella was five months old when I finally began to write again. I went to the coffee shop by our house one evening and pulled out paper and a pen. But instead of returning to the half-finished pieces I had been writing before Stella's birth, I started to write about the single most life-changing experience of my life: becoming a mother. I began with an image: my daughter, writhing on white blankets, beamed from the NICU into the television set in my hospital room days after she was born. As soon as that image was down on paper, other images followed. After an hour, there were tears in my eyes, and words covering the page. And for the first time since my daughter was born, the world felt a little bigger, and I felt a little less alone. Just getting those memories down on paper made me feel lighter.

In the following weeks, I continued to write about Stella's birth and hospitalization, and with each passing month, I felt healthier and more grounded; I was doing the only thing I knew how to do to make sense of what happened to me, to us—I was writing again.

When I returned to school in the fall, this writing became my thesis and later a completed manuscript. But when I began to talk about my new project, I encountered a number of raised eyebrows and glazed eyes. One person even said, "Oh, you're writing about your baby? How, um, sweet." I began to realize that some people were not taking my writing seriously because my subject matter had to do with motherhood. They didn't seem to think it was a subject worthy of real literature.

When you say you're writing about "motherhood" some people assume that the story—if indeed there is any story at all—will consist only of sleepless nights, diaper changes, nursing debacles, and tantruming toddlers. They assume if they opened your book they would be sucked into the minutiae of daily life with children.

This reminds me of something that poet Deborah Garrison said when I interviewed her a few years ago, after her second collection of poetry, *The Second Child,* was published. I asked whether responses to this collection differed from responses to her first collection, *Working Girl,* and she said, "I think that motherhood as a subject can blind people. They are distracted by it—they have ideas about what motherhood poetry should or shouldn't be—and sometimes they can't get past this to really see the way a poem was constructed."

So even while I was writing the first draft of my memoir, I knew I was involved in an uphill battle to get it taken seriously. But this was a book I was passionate about writing, one I felt deserved to be out in the world. My solution was to keep writing, and also to develop a creative nonfiction class for women interested in writing about *their* experiences as mothers. I wanted to create a place where women could give written expression to their lives as mothers, where motherhood writing would be taken seriously as art, where it would be supported and critiqued. I also started a blog on which I began promoting and reviewing motherhood literature and interviewing authors.

Through my blog and teaching I discovered exactly what I expected: women—mothers—crafting memoirs and essays dealing with issues of identity, loss and longing, neurosis and fear, ambivalence and joy. I found stories about transformation and how the authors see themselves in relation to the world in which they live. Last time I checked, this was the stuff of which real literature was made.

Reading about other mothers' lives and experiences has expanded my world. To be able to walk in someone else's shoes, whether it's for a moment or an hour or a few days, is an incredible gift. I have gained insight into parenting and the human experience.

The stories I've read and listened to have ranged from light and funny to heartbreaking, and there is room for all of these stories as a part of motherhood literature.

In the introduction to their anthology *Mothers: Twenty Stories of Contemporary Motherhood*, Kathleen Hirsch and Katrina Kenison write, "It takes courage to write about motherhood in a culture that sets women with children on the sidelines, and it takes even greater courage to give voice to the powerful emotions and fears that swirl deep beneath the surface of our daily lives, informing and shaping our relationships with our children and the world at large."

We all have stories to tell. Whether we tell these stories is another question. It *does* take courage to write about motherhood, to explore writing about our children and our roles as mothers, to "give voice to the emotions and fears that swirl deep beneath the surface" of our daily lives.

I hope this book will help give you the courage to get your mother stories down on paper. How often have you said, "Use your words!" to your children? How often have you heard other parents utter that phrase? Now it's *your* turn. I designed this book to help guide you on your journey as a mother writer and help you find the most effective way to tell the stories you need to tell.

How to Use This Book

Each chapter focuses on an aspect of craft—character, voice, structure, and so on—or a topic specific to mother writers, and builds on what was discussed in the previous chapters, using the writing of a wide range of mother writers as examples. The readings, writing instruction, and writing exercises included in each chapter are intended to be jumping-off points for your own writing. I encourage you to move through the book at your own pace. Take time to reflect on the readings and try one of the writing exercises before you move on to the next chapter.

Not all of the pieces used in the book will resonate with you, and that's OK. But try to identify what about the piece worked or didn't work for you. Identifying the "why" will help you with your own writing. The reading questions (in the Appendix) might be helpful as you think about how certain pieces are crafted.

Writing exercises are embedded in each chapter. There are also additional writing prompts in the Appendix if you feel you need more. You may also find that there is a line or an idea in one of the essays or poems that sparks your interest and sends you to your notebook or computer. Go where you're drawn. This is *your* writing.

My hope is that you will get started on a number of pieces as you work your way through this book, and that when you finish it, you will have enough momentum to keep going. It's wonderful if you can write a little bit each week, but I don't believe you need to write every day to be a writer, and as a mother, I know that writing can be difficult to fit into your day. But as you begin this journey as a mother writer, think about when and where you can squeeze writing into your life. Maybe you have one hour every Friday morning. Maybe you have 20 minutes three times a week as you wait to pick up your children from preschool or soccer practice. If you work outside the home, maybe you can go somewhere quiet on your lunch break and write twice a week. Be realistic about planning your writing time and be flexible. If you miss a day or a week, don't worry; there's always tomorrow.

Flannery O'Connor said, "I write to discover what I know." I agree. Writing is an act of discovery. Taking the time to sit down with pen and paper (or a laptop) can give you the space you need to discover what you think about the transformations inherent in motherhood. The more you write, the more you will understand what you know. So grab a cup of coffee or herbal tea (or a glass of wine!), find a quiet (or not so quiet) place to sit, and join me on this mother–writing journey.

CHAPTER 1

GETTING STARTED

THE DAY I WAS DISCHARGED FROM THE HOSPITAL after Stella was born, I stood over the warming table where my daughter lay baking under phototherapy lights and I began to sob, "This isn't fair. It wasn't supposed to happen this way." The nurse on duty patted me on the shoulder and said, "I know, but this is your birth story, and you need to accept it."

The only way I was able to do this—to accept our birth story and the trauma associated with it—was to write. And in writing our story, I was able to let go of it so I could focus on the important work of mothering my daughter.

But where to begin? It can be daunting to sit with a new document open on your computer screen. The blinking cursor seems to be saying *think faster, think faster!* Even a blank piece of paper is enough to make many a writer decide it's time—right this minute—to rearrange the spice cupboard or iron their underwear.

I think the easiest place to begin writing your mother stories is with a detail, an image. It was with one or two sensory details that I began writing my memoir: the image of my daughter writhing on a blanket on her open warming bed; the sickly-sweet smell of the NICU. These are the details that helped me dive into my narrative.

Concrete, sensory details are details that arise from our senses: sound, taste, smell, touch, sight. These are the details that allow us to step into an author's world, to feel as though we are walking in her shoes.

When I wrote about the first time I saw Stella in the NICU two days after she was born, I could have written: "I stare down at my tiny baby and feel sick to my stomach." Instead, I wrote this:

> I look down at her, and my stomach or chest—something in my center—tightens. A white ventilator is taped over her mouth, scrawny legs are splayed like a frog's, goggles cover her eyes, purple veins track across her skull like a spider web.
>
> I take a deep breath. *This cannot be my baby. This is not how it's supposed to happen.* I look up, around the large room: nurses hovering over incubators, monitors beeping, alarms sounding. Through the windows at the end of the room the sky is blue, bright fall blue. *How can that be? How can my baby be here, in this place? How can the sun be shining outside?*

The line, "I stare down at my tiny baby and feel sick to my stomach," is a summary-type sentence that would have done little to draw the reader into the scene. In contrast, the paragraphs above describe my daughter, the NICU, and my in-the-moment reactions. I hope these paragraphs allow the reader to enter the NICU and stand with me over the frame of my tiny daughter. I must assume that most readers haven't had a premature baby, and it's my job as a writer to ground my writing with enough detail so a reader can experience at least a little of that world.

Using concrete sensory details in your writing is an effective way to draw readers into your scene and story. Chitra Divakaruni does just this in the following essay:

Common Scents

. . . .

It's a cool December morning halfway across the world in Gurap, a little village outside Calcutta where we've come to visit my mother. I sit on the veranda and watch my little boys, Anand and Abhay, as they play on the dirt road. They have a new cricket bat and ball, a gift from their grandma, but soon they abandon these to feed mango leaves to the neighbor's goat, which has wandered over. Abhay, who is 2, wants to climb onto the goat's back. Anand, who is 5 and very much the big brother, tells him it's not a good idea, but Abhay doesn't listen.

Behind me the door opens. Even before I hear the *flap-flap* of her leather *chappals*, I know who it is. My mother, fresh from her bath, heralded by the scent of the sandalwood soap she has been using ever since I can remember. Its clean, familiar smell pulls me back effortlessly into my childhood.

When I was young, my mother and I had a ritual every evening. She would comb my hair, rub in hibiscus oil and braid it into thick double plaits. It took a long time—there were a lot of knots to work through. But I was rarely impatient. I loved the sleepy fragrance of the oil (the same oil she used, which she sometimes let me rub into her hair). I loved, too, the rhythm of her hands, and the stories (each with its not-so-subtle moral) that she told me as she combed. The tale of Sukhu and Dukhu, the two sisters. The kind one gets the prince, the greedy one is eaten up by a serpent. Or the tale of the little cowherd boy who outwits the evil witch. Size and strength, after all, are no match for intelligence.

What is it about smells that lingers in our subconscious, comforting and giving joy, making real what would otherwise be wooden and wordy? I'm not sure. But I do know this: Every lesson that I remember from my childhood, from my mother, has a smell at its center.

The smell of turmeric, which she made into a paste with milk and rubbed into my skin to take away blemishes, reminds me to take pride in my appearance, to make the best of what nature has given me.

The smell of the rosewater-scented rice pudding she always made for New Year is the smell of hope. It reminds me to never give up. Who knows—something marvelous may be waiting just around the bend.

Even the smell of the iodine she dabbed on my scraped knees and elbows, which I so hated then, is one I now recall with wry gratitude. Its stinging, bitter-brown odor is that of love, love that sometimes hurts while it's doing its job.

Let me not mislead you. I wasn't always so positively inclined toward my mother's lessons—or the smells that accompanied them. When I first moved to the United States, I wanted to change myself, completely. I washed every last drop of hibiscus oil from my hair with Vidal Sassoon shampoo. I traded in my saris for Levi's and tank tops. I danced the night away in discos and returned home in the bleary-eyed morning smelling of vodka and sweat and cigarettes, the perfume of young America.

But when Anand was born, something changed. They say you begin to understand your mother only when you become a mother yourself. Only then do you appreciate all the little things about her that you took for granted. Maybe that's true. Otherwise, that morning in the hospital, looking down at Anand's fuzzy head, why did I ask my husband to make a trip to the Indian store and bring me back a bar of sandalwood soap?

I have my own rituals now, with my boys, my own special smells that are quite different. (I learned early that we can't be our mothers. Most times, it's better to not even try.)

On weekends I make a big chicken curry with turmeric and cloves. Anand helps me cut up the tomatoes into uneven wedges; Abhay finger-shreds the cilantro with great glee. As the smell of spices fills the house, we sing. Sometimes it's a song from India:

Ay, ay, Chanda mama—Come to me, Uncle Moon. Sometimes it's "Old MacDonald Had a Farm."

When the children are sick, I sprinkle lavender water on a handkerchief and lay it on their foreheads to fend off that other smell, hot and metallic: the smell of fever and fear.

If I have a special event coming up, I open the suitcase my mother gave me at my wedding and let them pick out an outfit for me, maybe a gold-embroidered kurta or a silk shawl. The suitcase smells of rose potpourri. The boys burrow into it and take deep, noisy breaths.

Am I creating memories for them? Things that will comfort them in the dark, sour moments that must come to us all at some time? Who knows—there is so much out of my own childhood that I've forgotten that I can only hope so.

"Watch out!" says my mother now, but it's too late. The goat, having eaten enough mango leaves, has decided to move on. He gives a great shrug, and Abhay comes tumbling off his back. He lies on the dirt for a moment, his mouth a perfect O of surprise, then runs crying to me. A twinge goes through me even as I hide my smile. A new lesson, this, since motherhood: how you can feel someone else's pain so sharply, like needles, in your own bones.

When I pick him up, Abhay buries his face in my neck and stays there a long time, even after the tears have stopped. Is he taking in the smell of my body? Is he going to remember the fragrance of the jabakusum oil that I asked my mother to rub into my hair last night, for old time's sake? I'm not sure. But I do know this—I've just gained something new, something to add to my scent-shop of memories: the dusty, hot smell of his hair, his hands pungent with the odor of freshly torn mango leaves.

Divakaruni allows us to enter a world that might be unfamiliar to us by grounding her writing in the senses. This ability to transport the reader, to open a world that would otherwise be foreign, lies in the use of concrete, sensory details: bat and ball, goat and mango leaves, the sound of her mother's *chappals* flapping on the floor.

Divakaruni is able to cover a lot of ground in this short piece because of how she structures it (a topic we'll revisit later in the book). The stage of the piece is her visit to see her mother in Gurap. This is where she begins and ends the piece—it's where the physical action of the piece is taking place. But within that frame, Divakaruni takes us back to her own childhood and the smells she associates with it. She takes us to New York, where as a college student she spends her nights dancing, returning home "smelling of vodka and sweat and cigarettes, the perfume of young America." Then we move to the hospital when she becomes a mother herself, and to the rituals she is creating for her own sons. Then we are back in Gurap, watching Abhay fall from the goat. She is able to move around so much in time by staying focused on the topic at hand—scents—and by grounding her writing in detail.

For me, this piece is about love—Divakaruni's love for her mother and her sons and their love for her. We know exactly how she feels, but notice that she never uses the phrase "I felt..." She doesn't need to, because we understand how she feels through her use of details, which, as Divakaruni says in the piece, "make real what would otherwise be wooden and wordy."

Being concrete is especially important when we're writing about babies and children because it keeps our writing from becoming sentimental. We want to convey emotion and experience, but still make our writing real enough so that someone else can step into the world we create on the page. Whenever you find yourself using abstract words—those slippery concepts like love, hate, joy—stop and instead try to convey emotion through details.

PUTTING PEN TO PAPER—
APPROACHING THE WRITING EXERCISES

There are a couple of different ways to approach the writing exercises in this book. You can free-write or list or cluster. It doesn't matter how your words get onto paper or your computer; just get them down. I'll describe these different approaches below, but the thing to remember with each method is to turn off your internal editor. Suppressing that censorious voice will allow your mind to make associations and discoveries. Don't worry about spelling or grammar or who might someday read what you're writing. You don't need to show it to anyone. It's yours alone.

Free-writing
To free-write, you may want to set a timer for 15 to 20 minutes and write anything that comes to mind from an exercise or a reading. Do this without stopping, without deleting, without second-guessing yourself. I call this vomiting, which is my way to trick myself into not censoring or editing. Whatever comes out, comes out.

Clustering
This is the same idea as free-writing, but the writing comes out in a different form. This is a free-association process that can help you get started or become unstuck if you hit a wall with your writing. Start with a word in the center of your page and circle it. From there, let your mind wander, and jot down other words or phrases until you have a tree of circled words. (See the Appendix for a visual representation.) Once you have clustered around a topic, you may want to choose one thing from your cluster on which to free-write.

Listing
This approach is similar to clustering, but instead of creating a tree of words, you are making lists. Pick a topic and make a list of any related

ideas, words, or memories that pop into your mind. When you've completed a list on a certain topic, go back to it and choose one of the words or memories and expand on it with a free-write or another list. For instance, early in the process of writing my memoir, I made lists of details I didn't want to forget from Stella's stay in the hospital: the wall of photos of NICU graduates that led to the NICU, the way the afternoon light slanted through the blinds in the nursery in the days before Stella was discharged. Let your mind wander and see what happens.

WRITING EXERCISE:
SENSORY DETAILS AS A WAY TO BEGIN

As Divakaruni showed us, focusing on a sensory detail can help you find a way into your writing, into the story you need to tell. Now it's your turn: Think about the time when your child (or one of your children) was born, when she first arrived home, or even before she was born. If you adopted your child, maybe you want to focus on the first time you saw her photo. Is there a certain smell, sound, taste, texture, or picture that comes to mind? Start with that. Write it down. What other concrete details do you remember? Let your mind wander. Jump from image to image. Try to use as many sensory, concrete details as you can. Don't pick up your pen—just keep moving it across the paper—and don't worry about grammar or spelling.

If those early days and months feel too far removed, choose another period in your child's life that seemed particularly vivid to you, and begin writing details from that time.

WRITING EXERCISE:
AMBUSHED BY A SMELL

The summer after my freshman year in college I worked for a large adhesive-manufacturing company. (I know. I know. It was actually that summer that made me realize I did not, in fact, want to be a chemist. I spent my lunch breaks sitting outside on the manicured lawn reading Hemingway.) Anyway, the building where I had to perform my adhesive tests had a distinctive smell—an odd combination of chemicals and adhesive and burnt rubber. I was around this smell all summer, and I actually grew to enjoy it, but because I decided to go into the humanities rather than the sciences, I didn't smell it again for years. Then, one day in my mid-thirties while walking down the street, I took a deep breath and there it was. I had no idea where it was coming from, but I was suddenly 19 years old again, carefully lining up adhesive strips on metal plates.

Our sense of smell is the sense most closely associated with memory, and it has the power to transport us to another time. Some of my students have described being ambushed by smells that yank them back into their childhood: cigar smoke took one student back to her grandfather's living room; walking past a boxwood shrub took another student to her grandmother's garden. Make a list of smells that have the power to transport you to another time. Choose one smell and describe it in as much detail as possible. Then describe the memories and emotions that this smell evokes.

A Moment in Time
One thing that often leads us to write about our children is a need
not to forget. Time goes so quickly, and suddenly our children are no
longer fussy infants; they are building rockets in the living room out of
cardboard and tinfoil; they are writing notes on their bedroom doors
telling everyone to "KEEP OUT!" The years pass so fast (even when
certain days seem to be without end). The following poem by Linda
Lee Crosfield captures the bittersweet feeling of the passing years, of
needing to let her son go out into the world:

Packing the Car

he packs the car with memories
his, not mine
in crates and boxes he takes
from the house like evidence
removed from the scene of a crime

I watch as he stands back
surveys his work
his eyes narrow
and he leans into the car
adjusts a box this way
turns another on its side
making everything fit
making room for just one more

as I watch him I remember
the first jigsaw puzzle we did together
I kept putting his hand on the right piece
showing him how best to place it
here

or here
until he frowned and said
he could do it himself
and did

I stand aside
watch helplessly
as books stream from shelves
into boxes, out the door
and I envy them their invitation
to accompany him on this journey
to the rest of his life

gradually I'll notice little things
the phone will stop being for him
there'll be one less toothbrush
by the bathroom sink
and milk will last longer than a day

but right now
the dog who's famous
for her big brown eyes
closes them tight
when he says goodbye
and her tail droops
lower than my heart
as tires crunch
against the gravel in the driveway
and he drives off
into the late summer morn

Like Divakaruni, Crosfield grounds us clearly in the stage of the poem, which takes place in the "now" of her watching her son pack for college. But I love how the past—helping that tiny version of her son with the puzzle—intrudes into the poem as well. And because she grounds us in the stage of the poem, she is also able to move forward and give us a glimpse of what her life will look like when he is gone.

One way to capture certain moments in your children's lives— memorializing them—is to write them down now, while they're still fresh in your mind. When I discussed this desire with Deborah Garrison a few years ago, she said:

> For me, the impulse for a poem arises out of a specific moment. It happens organically, but it's interesting because writing poetry is a way to chronicle some of the moments of my life and my children's lives. My youngest is now almost five, so when I look at some of the poems in *The Second Child*, I think, Oh, that's how it felt to nurse my son. It's amazing how much we do forget as parents. So by writing poetry, I am, in fact, fixing these moments in time so that they don't disappear altogether.

I think this is a powerful impulse for parents, for mothers—let us not forget—and it's interesting to contemplate how this idea works in our writing. What are the moments and memories that you don't want to forget?

WRITING EXERCISE: A MOMENT IN TIME

Think of a moment with your child or children that you do not want to forget. Write for 15 minutes and try to incorporate as many sensory, concrete details as you can. Where are you? What does the room look like? What are you doing? Be as physical in your descriptions as possible.

WRITING EXERCISE: LOOKING BACK

Crosfield brings the memory of working a puzzle with her son into the present action of her poem. If you have older children, what memories intrude on your "now" with your children? Do you have trouble reconciling who they are now with who they were as small children? Make a list of memories from when your children were young. Then describe a current scene with one of your children. How do the past versions of your children interact with how you see them now?

CHAPTER 2

CREATIVE NONFICTION
AND MOTHERHOOD

CREATIVE NONFICTION IS THE UMBRELLA TERM under which you can place memoir, personal essays, autobiography, collage, literary journalism, and lyric essays, to name a few. One of the things I love about it is that it's an open genre; it shifts and changes, and there is always room for new subgenres under that umbrella.

In his essay "Toward a Definition of Creative Nonfiction" from *The Fourth Genre: Contemporary Writers of/on Creative Nonfiction*, Bret Lott says, "We can no more understand what creative nonfiction is by trying to define it than we can learn how to ride a bike by looking at a bicycle tire, a set of handlebars, the bicycle chain itself." You must come to your definition experientially. The more you write creative nonfiction, the better sense you will have about what it is and what it is capable of doing.

The types of creative nonfiction I focus on in this book are memoir and personal essays—writing that uses the author's life to say something about the world in which she lives. Both of these forms use the techniques of poetry and fiction, such as lyrical language, metaphor, character development, scene, and dialogue. Both forms also often contain the following: reflection, an apparent subject and a deeper subject, attention to craft, and universal themes.

Reflection

Reflection is the author making sense of what she's experiencing; she is thinking on the page, trying to process and make sense of her lived experiences. She is struggling for honesty and searching for meaning. The inclusion of you—the writer, the narrator—in your writing is one of the things that makes a piece of writing memoir. This is important to keep in mind when we're writing about our children. Bret Lott says that creative nonfiction is "writing about oneself *in relation to* the subject at hand." Sometimes we think we're writing an essay about our children, and indeed, they provide the situation. But ultimately, I think you'll find that most often you are writing about you *in relation to* your children. Or you are simply using motherhood as a lens to talk about something larger. (We'll discuss reflection in depth in Chapter 9.)

An apparent subject and a deeper subject

Vivian Gornick, in her book *A Situation and a Story: The Art of Personal Narrative*, says that "every work of literature has both a situation and a story. The situation is the context or circumstance, sometimes the plot; the story is the emotional experience that preoccupies the writer." The story is what the piece of writing is really about.

For instance, my memoir is about Stella's premature birth, but that's merely the situation of the book. The real story is about navigating the dark side of motherhood and learning to live with uncertainty. It's a story of faith, friendship, family, and the power of narrative to connect us to one another.

Attention to craft

There is attention to language, character development, dialogue, place, metaphor, and structure. I want concrete sensory details; I want to be able to see and hear the characters you're writing about; I want to have a sense of place.

Universal themes

Regardless of the story you're telling, there is some universal aspect to it, something to which readers can relate even if their stories are completely different from your own. One of my students remarked that sometimes our stories feel so exceptional that it's challenging to see beyond our experiences and find the universal themes that will resonate with readers. I agree, and this is why it's important to identify the deeper subject in our writing. When we are able to articulate the real story in our writing, we automatically find ourselves pushing toward universals. (Often the universals are already there, but they might not be fully realized on the page yet.)

The story in memoir is often about a shift in perspective. What change did the narrator undergo as a result of these events? What does she understand about her life now? It is not a "this happened and then this happened" kind of writing. William Zinsser, author of *On Writing Well: The Classic Guide to Writing Nonfiction*, says, "Unlike autobiography, which moves in a dutiful line from birth to fame, memoir narrows the lens, focusing on a time in the writer's life that was unusually vivid, such as childhood or adolescence, or that was framed by war or public service or some other special circumstance."

Motherhood is exactly the kind of "special circumstance" that lends itself to memoir. It is a time of transition and sometimes a period of intense identity struggle: Who am I if I spend all day shirtless, trying to nurse a colicky baby? What happened to my former life, my former self? How do I balance my own needs with those of my family?

I am drawn to all kinds of motherhood memoirs because I am interested in the different ways that women process the challenges and joys of motherhood, and how they write about life in general through their mother eyes. Debra Gwartney, author of *Live Through This: A Mother's Memoir of Runaway Daughters and Reclaimed Love,* says, "A well-written book [about motherhood] is going to say something profound about the human condition, and we need to hear the voices of women who can express the plight we're all in as humans."

WRITING AS AN ACT OF DISCOVERY

I'd like to return to the Flannery O'Connor quote from the Introduction: "I write to discover what I know." As you begin work on the writing exercises, you may come up against the failings of your memory. We must work our way through our memories when we write. We question, we wonder, and hopefully in the end we realize what we need to say.

As you begin to write, don't expect the *stories* of your pieces to be fleshed out yet. You might have simply a glimmer of the true story. This is where you should be when you're writing a first draft. In her essay "Memory and Imagination," Patricia Hampl says that a first draft is a first draft because "I haven't yet gotten to know it, haven't given it a chance to tell me anything." Sometimes we have an idea about what we want to write. Maybe we sit down and write diligently. We finish the piece and go back to work on grammar and language. But the piece doesn't ring true; there's still something missing. This often happens because, Hampl says, the piece "hasn't yet found its subject; it isn't yet about what it wants to be about. Note: What *it* wants, not what *I* want." You can help your pieces be what they need to be by asking: What is the heart of this piece? If you can't yet tell what this the piece is about, ask: What are the most interesting parts of the piece? Where do the possibilities lie? Where do I need more writing?

YOUR VERSION OF THE TRUTH

When I pick up a memoir, I trust that the writer has written her truth to the best of her ability. And I mean *her* truth, not a capital-T truth. You will remember events differently than the other people in your life do, even if they experienced the same events. Each of these versions is valid because memoir is about the relationship between the subject (what happened) and the narrator. That is where the story lies. But it is also possible to interrogate the reliability of our memories as we write and in our writing. Notice how Jill Christman does this in the following essay:

Three Takes on a Jump

Take One
I am five. We live on an island off the coast of Massachusetts and I want to jump off the roof of our one-story house and into the sand. My mother's boyfriend, a deep-sea fisherman by the name of Captain Bill with red hair and a boat named after my mother, says no, I may not jump off the roof. From here, the golden sand looks deceptively soft. Like a pillow. Almost springy. I am five and I want to jump.

This is a favorite story from the maritime era of our family history—right up there with the half-roasted turkey flying from the oven on Captain Bill's boat and sliding around the pitching galley like a greased pig and the lobsters knotted onto the Christmas tree by a nautical Santa. (I claim the lobsters were alive—shimmying crustaceans! salty elves!—but everybody else says boiled. Were they red? I cannot remember. I remember their wiggling claws shaking the branches.)

Like the turkey and the lobsters, the house-jumping story has been told and retold until everybody is sure of the details, the way it all went down. Today, I am not so sure. Sitting around a picnic table thirty years after the fact, I mention to my partially assembled family that there's a thing called "shareability"—the reason we all know the details of the jumping story is because we've been refining the script for years, sharing the story. The story we think we know has more to do with the telling, and retelling, than it does with memory. In other words, ours is a corroborative tale produced with all the witnesses in the same room—except, in this case, I realize I was the only one who was there, the only actual witness, and the story I'm hearing might not be the one I remember. *It's called shareability,* I say. For this piece of psychological trivia, I am eyed skeptically over the lips of beer bottles.

Everybody knows the person who makes up stories in *this* family and it's sure not them. I'm the hero in the shared version so I should just let it rest, let it fly, but in my line of work, these things matter, and all I'm saying is we need to look into the gaps here. For example, what am I doing on the roof in the first place? What fool let a five-year-old climb a ladder, scale the warm, black shingles, peer down into the sand and consider jumping? How did I get there? I am five!

But let the picnic table family finish the story. On the roof I am, and I am *insisting* on jumping down. There is a stand off. Finally, the sea captain boyfriend says *Go ahead.* This is everybody's favorite part and everybody but me chimes in like a Greek chorus (after all, as the subject of the story, the little girl with all the chutzpah, somehow my participation would be unseemly). *Go ahead,* he said. He never thought she'd actually do it, never, but Jill didn't hesitate. She marched, she *marched,* right to the edge of the roof and jumped off. She landed like a sack of potatoes—*a sack of potatoes!*—in the sand and then, and then, she stood right up, brushed off her pants and said, "There."

There!

There.

Take Two

Okay, so this is the roof-jumping story I remember and I'm foolish to do so, because in this version I spin myself as a victim instead of a hero, a girl who is desperate instead of tough. In memory, I am older than five. Seven or maybe even eight. Same house, same roof, same sand. My brother and his pack of boys feature here. Let's say there are four of them all together, all older than me, all utterly antagonistic. There are no adults in this story. The boys have climbed on the roof and pulled the ladder up. I want them to slide the ladder down so I can climb up, too. They refuse. They're taunting me. I'm the girl, the baby, the worthless, whiny one. Then, my brother lowers the ladder down to me. *Alright,* he says, *come on up.* Oh joy! I am part of the pack! I am nearly a boy! I scamper up and hurry to the peak of the roof. I can see the ocean from here!

The boys scuttle down the ladder like cockroaches down the side of a refrigerator, flipping the ladder down into the sand as the last one reaches solid ground. It was a trick. I am stuck. Hours pass. Soon, darkness will fall. The boys come and go, but now the talk turns to sand monsters and other creatures of the beach night. I no longer want to be up. I want to be down. I beg, I plead. They laugh. This is such a good one.

At some point, the boys toss up a garbage bag: large, black, Hefty. They want to know whether the bag will work as a parachute. The bag is my only way down. I cannot remember how long I wait. Finally, I shake out the bag, hold the edges rolled tight in both fists. I am hopeful the air will come in to break my fall.

This story has a moral: A garbage bag does *not* work as a parachute. Don't try it.

There is no "there!" here. I land, I hurt, I cry. I tell on the creeps when my mother gets home.

Take Three

No third version exists, although this same black roof has featured in decades of failed dreams in which my featherless arms move in futile wing beats and I cannot fly (do I lack confidence?). But there is the thing I *know* to be true: I *did* jump off that roof and into the sand. My body remembers what it feels like to hit.

Sand is not as soft as it looks. Sand, when arrived at from a height of at least ten feet—Hefty bag or no—receives its guest with only slightly more benevolence than concrete. Sand is ground rock, after all. When I hit, the air left my lungs like a balloon clapped between two bricks. I felt the blow, the sharp emptying of my lungs and then their refusal to fill again. Chest down, lifting my face from the sand, grit in my eyes, my nose, stuck to my lips, I could not breathe. No matter whose version is true, I hadn't expected this. I was sure the sand would be soft, or at least softer. I was a child.

Christman questions the different versions of this event, and I love how she differentiates her and her family members' memories of what happened from what she knows for sure: she did jump and it did hurt. How much do your versions of certain events differ from the versions of your family members?

WRITING EXERCISE:
WHAT YOU DON'T KNOW FOR SURE

Even as we become more in touch with our memories through writing, some memories still elude us. When I began working on my memoir, the early days of Stella's life were difficult for me to remember (partly because I was overwhelmed and partly because I was being administered copious amounts of pain and antiseizure medication). One way I was able to get around my lack of memory was to write what I didn't remember. Every time I got stuck with writing those early days, I started another line with "I don't remember..." For instance, "I don't remember what she looked like when she was held to my face." Even though I don't remember this detail, the fact that I don't remember it adds to the story.

Think of a time about which your memories are fuzzy. Set aside 15 to 20 minutes to free-write. Each time your memory fails you, write, "I don't remember..." How does this lead you into your memories in a new way?

Did this exercise change the feel of your memories? Did you unearth anything that surprised you?

WRITING EXERCISE:
A MOMENT OF FASCINATION

The things that obsess and fascinate us can be effective jumping–off points for our writing. (Think of Christman trying to get to the bottom of what really happened the day she jumped off the roof.) Is there something (a moment, a memory, a relationship) that nags at you, that you don't fully understand? (This can have to do with parenting, or your own family of origin, or it could be about something totally different.) Describe it in as much detail as possible. Then begin interrogating it as Christman does in "Three Takes." Why does it continue to nag at you? What do you know for sure? What still don't you understand? Where does this questioning lead you?

CHAPTER 3

MOTHERHOOD MYTHS
AND MODELS

WHILE I WAS PREGNANT, I IMAGINED EARLY motherhood would be filled with blissful hours holding and nursing my daughter. I dreamt of lazy afternoons, napping alongside her in our bed. (I even—foolishly—thought I would be able to drink a latte and write at the coffeeshop as she slept next to me in her car seat.) Instead, hours of attempted nursing left us both in tears, her constant crying (which we later learned was the result of gastroesophageal reflux) shredded my nerves, and I longed to escape the confines of our small house. I was left feeling that there was something wrong with me, that I was failing at motherhood.

From working with and talking to hundreds of mothers, I know my feelings of failure weren't unique. I know women who feel they failed because they abandoned their natural birth plan because of pain, exhaustion, or danger to their babies. I know women who, after struggling with breast-feeding for weeks or months, eventually switched to formula, but couldn't forgive themselves for not succeeding at something that was supposed to be "natural." I know women who struggled to adjust to parenting a child with additional needs, and those who simply struggled to balance the sometimes all-encompassing role of motherhood with their own needs and interests.

Even as our culture sets "women with children on the sidelines," as Hirsch and Kenison write in their anthology *Mothers: Twenty Stories of Contemporary Motherhood*, the cultural narratives of motherhood prevalent in our society seem to say that motherhood is innate, that it will come naturally, that it is the most important thing women can do. That's a lot of pressure, and I think many of us internalize these expectations and values. And if motherhood unfolds differently than we expect, we may be left floundering, wondering what is wrong with us.

As we write about our experiences as mothers, it's important to acknowledge both the cultural narratives of motherhood—expectations, ideals, myths—and come to terms with our opinions about what it means to be a "good mother."

To do this, I think it's helpful to think back to the ways you were mothered. Some of my students have written about their "perfect" moms and their struggles as new mothers to deal with this ideal modeled for them as children. Some students have written about absent mothers and mothers who didn't mother them the way they needed. Here is an example of the latter by Lucinda Cummings:

My Mother Is Missing

My mother was a pretty mother, a youthful, stylish mother who colored her hair, smoked cigarettes, and read novels by the sackful. At the public library, she checked out modern sculptures and paintings, and displayed them in our living room. She wanted her children to make her laugh.

My mother used to be a party girl, the belle of the ball, indulged by her parents. She became a child mother, offended by the pain of childbirth, furious at her abandonment by callous nurses and doctors who did not understand she needed pampering. My mother said my older brother came into the world angry on the hottest day in July, but it was she who was angry, at the world.

My mother hated to cook, regarded housework as superfluous. She loved to sunbathe in her turquoise bikini in our back yard. She was a rebel mother, a mother who took us to the Unitarian church and to Quaker meetings when our Methodist grandparents questioned our lack of religious training. She was a smart mother who went back to college with four children at home. She majored in sociology, studied late into the night, accepted only A's. We sat in the back seat of the station wagon while she drove around our neighborhood, placing her sociological surveys into every third mailbox. She became a working mother, bought herself a red Austin-Healey, fell asleep on the sofa every Friday after work. My mother was a Southern mom who volunteered for Eugene McCarthy, taught in an all-black public school, wrote letters to the city council, read Betty Friedan. She told us we were free to choose our own politics and religion when we grew up.

My mother was a yelling mother. She couldn't make my younger brother come home on time, do his homework, or stay inside his neighborhood boundaries. She screamed at him, made him sit in the corner, told him he must follow the rules, but secretly didn't want him to. She called him her "Sunshine," he made her laugh, he was her rebel child.

My mother was a crying mother, emerging from the bathroom with red eyes, a mother in her bedroom with the blinds drawn and the door closed. She was a mother on medication; a mother who forgot important things, like my lunch money; a mother in the hospital; a mother who didn't share my enthusiasm for my first spelling book. She was a mother who didn't volunteer at school or socialize with the other mothers. A mother who drank ten cups of instant coffee every day. When she was too depressed to work, she left her job and stayed at home, making enormous tapestries out of bright yarns and burlap, and reading women's magazines. I looked elsewhere for someone to admire.

When my mother came to stay with me after the birth of my second child, she sat at my table drinking coffee and told me the same stories of my childhood over and over. She held my newborn son, letting his head flop over her arm unsupported. When Benjamin, my four-year-old, came home from preschool, she made only the smallest effort to engage him. She lost track of time, and took no initiative to do what needed to be done around my house. Sleep deprived and overwhelmed, I could no longer count on the well of compassion and forbearance that had always covered my anger; it was suddenly dry. She sat. I seethed.

What was it about that visit that caused all my patience to abandon me, leaving me with only the urge to scream at my mother? After all, I'd covered all of this in therapy: cried about it, screamed about it, analyzed it and wrapped it up in neat little packages labeled "maternal depression," "caretaking childhood." Why was I then furious with her incompetence and her inadequate mothering, when nothing had changed between us? I could have focused on positive mothering role models: my grandmother, my aunt, other women I knew; but I didn't. It was my own mother I wanted, and she was missing, again. My mother's visit reminded me of what I did not get as a child, what I vowed to give to my children, what suddenly felt impossible to deliver, especially with two children.

Benjamin had struggled to adjust to his new baby brother's arrival. On the first day we were home from the hospital, he "accidentally" let the upstairs bathtub overflow, sending a deluge through the living room ceiling. Whenever I nursed the baby, Benjamin needed something, and he could not wait. He screamed at me, lay on the floor, red faced, kicking his feet. I had worked so hard at giving him the nurturing I missed, and I knew I was disappointing him. Every word he hurled at me pierced another hole in my mothering confidence.

After my mother left, depression came to stay. I became the sad mom, the crying mom behind the closed door. I held my nursing newborn in the night. As we rocked, I peeled back layers of self-doubt, anger toward my mother, and guilt over being angry. Finally I came to this: somehow I had counted on healing my childhood self by being the mother to my children that I never had. But if my mother was this incompetent at mothering me, how could I possibly have inside me what it took to be a good mother to my sons? I visualized myself as a newborn, cradled in her arms with my head flopping over, and I burst into tears. All of the ways in which I'd raised myself flooded over me, and I stared into what I imagined was the dark void in myself, the deep gulf that would never hold enough sustenance for my boys to grow up whole. Hope felt impossible, for my sons and for myself.

In the end, my way out of despair was through the wise observation of my therapist: "We often grow up to be the best possible parents to the child that we once were, rather than the child we have." My parenting of Benjamin would have made me the ideal mother to myself as a child: empathic, attuned, responding predictably, meeting every need. But I was far from the ideal mother to Benjamin. Yes, he needed the nurturing and empathy, but he also needed limits and the chance to learn how to wait, to tolerate frustration, to entertain himself, and to share his mother with his new brother.

Over many months, I worked hard at balancing the needs of my two children. Sometimes I had to practice saying no, meaning what I said, and living with Benjamin's frustration, tantrum by tantrum. At other times, my task was to care for myself, by giving myself time alone, creative outlets, solid boundaries, and time with women friends who made me feel whole; in short, nurturing the child within myself, so that I no longer needed to do it by indulging my children. For some of us, these lessons are learned early in life, from our mothers, and they become a natural part of us that emerges as we enter parenthood. But for others, like myself, these are hard-won lessons, forged in the fires of postpartum depression and learning from our mistakes.

. . . .

Cummings tries to come to terms with how she was mothered and what effect this had on her own mothering. One of my students commented that the use of repetition was effective in adding to the complexity of Cummings's mother: "She didn't try to sum her up in one sentence but instead spent a paragraph on each attribute or group of attributes. I think we are all complex, and that no one is all horrible or all perfect."

Another student pointed out that the repetition in the piece is "an effective way of knitting together a series of the same behaviors that might not have happened sequentially (instead of 'and then, and then')." I agree, and I think that Cummings's piece can be a model for how to convey events that happened regularly in the past.

One of the things I find so compelling about this essay is the way it shifts from how Cummings perceived her mother had failed to how she felt she was failing as a mother to her sons. This idea of being a failure or "bad" mother can be an insidious force in our lives and can shape how we perceive our abilities as mothers. When we write about motherhood, it's helpful to try to identify when and how these ideas made their way into our consciousness.

WRITING EXERCISE:
PUTTING FAILURE IN PERSPECTIVE

Make a list of moments when you felt like a bad or failing mother. Pick one and write about it in as much detail as possible, including your emotional reaction to the scene. Now take a step back. Can you identify where your feelings of failure are rooted (cultural expectation, expectations you have of yourself, your own experiences in your family of origin)? Write for another 10 minutes, trying to get to the bottom of where these feelings came from. Then look back at your original scene. Has your perspective of that moment shifted?

WRITING EXERCISE:
MOTHERHOOD MODELS

Take a few minutes and describe your mother. If you didn't have a mother growing up, did someone else play a mothering role in your life? Describe her. Maybe you didn't feel you had a "good" mother and maybe you didn't know anyone who fit this description. So what would a "good" mother look like? How did/does this ideal affect your own parenting? How have you parented your own child the same or differently?

FORGIVING OUR MOTHERS

A few years ago at a writing conference, I listened to a panel of authors who contributed to the anthology *Riding Shotgun: Women Write About Their Mothers* discuss their work. One of the writers, Carrie Pomeroy, described how the process of writing her essay "Aftereffects" allowed her to forgive her mother, who had been depressed and angry and struggling after the death of Pomeroy's father when Pomeroy was a teenager. One thing Pomeroy did as she was trying to get a three-dimensional version of her mother on the page was to "brainstorm and free-write about three thematic areas" where she had "many associations, images, and memories" of her mother. For Pomeroy, these were: dancing, food/eating, and housework. As she wrote about these thematic areas, she found she was able to access another side of her mother, one not tainted by her early widowhood. And in the process of better understanding her mother, she was able to forgive her. You may want to try a similar exercise.

WRITING EXERCISE:
MOTHER ASSOCIATIONS

What are the thematic areas that you most strongly associate with your mother or mother model? Make a list of them, pick one area, and free-write or cluster on that topic for 15 minutes. Then pick another, and another. When you're finished, step back and look at what you've written. Did writing your mother or mother model in this way change how you perceive her or help you gain insight into her as a person?

PERHAPSING

Another way to approach writing about your mother is by "perhapsing." This is a phrase coined by Lisa Knopp in her essay "'Perhapsing': The Use of Speculation in Creative Nonfiction" from the online journal *Brevity*. Knopp writes:

> At some point, writers of creative nonfiction come to a road block or dead end in our writing, where we don't have access to the facts we need to tell our story or to sustain our reflection with depth and fullness. If only it was ethical to just make something up, we might think, or to elaborate a bit on what we know. But of course, then we wouldn't be writing creative nonfiction. It might appear that our choices in such cases are to either abandon the topic or write a thinly developed scene or reflection.

Knopp goes on to describe how we can use expressions like *perhaps, maybe, might have,* and *what if* to get at unknown possibilities in our stories without abandoning creative nonfiction. With the use of these words, readers are clued in to the fact that the writer is speculating. Knopp says:

> Perhapsing can be particularly useful when writing about childhood memories, which are often incomplete because of a child's limited understanding at the time of the event, and the loss of details and clarity due to the passage of time.

I think "perhapsing" is particularly helpful when you're not clear about another person's motivation. If there is something about your mother, her life, or your relationship with her that you don't understand or don't know, try the following exercise. This exercise is interesting as a way of deepening a scene or a memory for the reader, but it can also shift your perspective about someone or something. It can help us understand and be more empathetic toward the people in our lives.

WRITING EXERCISE:
"PERHAPSING" YOUR MOTHER

Make a list of memories you have of your mother in which her motivation was not clear to you. If you didn't know your mother, begin by writing the facts and details that you *do* know. Pick one of these moments or details to free-write for 15 minutes. Let yourself speculate, using "perhaps" or "maybe" or "I wonder." After you are finished, read what you've written. Did you open a new window of perspective? What still isn't clear?

CHAPTER 4

OUR CHILDREN AS CHARACTERS: CHARACTER DEVELOPMENT

YOU WANT YOUR READERS TO FEEL A CONNECTION
to the characters in your writing, and in order to make that happen, you
need to write them in enough detail so readers really know them. Sometimes when I mention that I'm working on character development with
my students, someone will say, "I thought you were teaching *non*fiction."
There is an assumption that because the people in a work of creative
nonfiction really exist, there is no need to concern ourselves with character development. But nonfiction writers need to write believable and
three-dimensional characters precisely *because* these characters are real
people; writing them accurately is a way to honor them. We also need to
think about character development when we are writing about ourselves.
How does the reader know us? How do we reveal who we really are?

One of the wonderful things about writing about our children is
that we, as writers, get to decide how the reader first "sees" them. What
do you want readers to notice first about your child? How do you get
readers invested in your children as characters? Keep these questions in
mind as you read the two pieces in this chapter.

Our character is revealed in the way we talk, how we dress, who and what we surround ourselves with, and what we believe and think. Some of who we are exists in our heads, what we are pondering—our worldview. But we also need to be physical people on the page.

It's challenging to write the people who are close to us, because we spend so much time with them that we take their gestures and faces and body language for granted—these things have become a part of us. When I began working on my memoir, I struggled to get my husband, Donny, down on paper in a way that made him come alive. When I was in front of my computer, I couldn't remember how he held his head, what his mouth did when he was nervous, and so on. I had to go home and study him, which was a little awkward. (Him: Why are you staring at me? Me: I'm not. Him: Yes, you are. Me: I just love you. Is that so wrong?)

In *Writing Down the Bones*, Natalie Goldberg says, "When we live in a place for too long, we grow dull. We don't notice what is around us." The same thing happens with the people in our lives. We must train ourselves to notice their gestures and speech patterns in order to write them effectively.

There are a number of ways to create believable, three-dimensional characters in your writing, to bring your children and spouses and friends and parents to life on the page. Here are a few elements to think about:

Speech/dialogue: What your characters say and how they say it reveals a lot about who they are. Think of the language that is specific to your family, and make a list of phrases that you come back to again and again. The way we speak and the phrases we use are hints to our characters. Think about tone and delivery as well.

Body language: This is something that we often overlook, especially when we are just beginning to write. Body language and how people hold themselves says so much about them. What do you know about me if I walk into a room full of people, slouched, not making eye contact? What if I slide against the wall instead of walking straight into a room?

What do you know about me if I walk upright, shoulders back, if I meet people's eyes and smile? Body language is an important part of dialogue and can be inserted in and around actual speech.

Backstory and summary: Part of who our characters are exists in the past, in history, and we can convey this with backstory. Backstory can enter into a piece of writing as a fully fleshed-out scene that took place in the past, or it can be a few lines of summary. Summary is a form of "telling" in which the narrator steps back and quickly encapsulates an event, action, or information for the reader. Summary can be an efficient way to get information about your characters to the reader.

As you're thinking about character, keep in mind all of the senses we talked about in the first chapter: smell, touch, sound, sight, taste. How does your baby smell? What sounds does your eight-year-old make when he's building a Lego city? Describe your daughter's expression when she's watching her favorite movie.

As you read the two essays in this chapter, notice the ways that each writer creates a sense of character. Can you point to specific ways that we know Jeremy and Beth in "The Line"? Toby and Sara in "Music in His Genes"? Here is Beth Kephart's "The Line Is White, and It Is Narrow":

The Line Is White, and It Is Narrow

The line gets drawn, and the line gets drawn again. There are, as they say, so many degrees of separation, so much growing up that must go on: The bottle replacing the breast. The book the child reads alone. Something whispered so that the mother cannot hear. Children retreat and return to us like the tide—tripping out beyond our reach, lapping back in, turning once more to greet the sea. They are discovering themselves, of course. But we are also discovering them.

* * *

Jeremy is eight when he decrees his love for all things soccer. He is at the kitchen table telling the sort of story that sends my stomach to my knees. It's a recess story, my least favorite kind. I'm not an optimist when it comes to recess.

"James and me were selling walnuts," Jeremy starts out earnestly, sparing me context, as he is wont to do, and peeling the cheap white paper from an ice cream sandwich. "Then we dug for China."

"Did you find it?" I ask.

"What?" Jeremy blinks. The ice cream sandwich has slouched. "China?"

"Of course not," Jeremy says; he has learned to be so patient with me. "We were just digging for it." He finishes his treat, and there he sits, slathered with white and dark-brown sugars.

"So then what happened?" My question: quiet and cautious.

"Some of the other kids were playing tag, but most of them were playing soccer. Second, third, fourth, and fifth graders. They're good. They really are."

"Uh-huh," I tell Jeremy. "Hmm."

"I love soccer," Jeremy says, with operatic emphasis. "I love it. I really do."

"You do?" I say, fumbling for a comeback to this unexpected outburst of passion for a sport we've never once discussed, read about, or watched on TV. "You love it even though you've never played?"

"Yup."

"Why?" I ask, genuinely stumped. "Why soccer?"

"Because I love it," Jeremy says. "And I'm going to play. I'm going to get my foot on the ball and I'm going to kick it. I just want to kick it, see what it feels like to kick the ball in a game of recess soccer. I'm going to play soccer. I'm going to be good." He looks at me with his huge, lit-up eyes, and I'm won over. I believe him, because I am his mom.

* * *

The next day, at pick-up time, there are two salty stripes that streak from the lower ledge of Jeremy's eyes to the cliff of his well-defined chin. He is forcing his bottom lip to stop quivering by pursing his pliant upper lip shut. "How was school?" I ask him, deflated at once by the sight of his sadness.

"Fine," he answers, nobly. "Just fine."

"Are you feeling sad?" He sits behind me because of the purported dangers of the car's safety air bags, and I turn around at the first red light to get another good look at him. Those are the vestiges of tears, for sure.

"Nope."

"Did something happen?"

Nothing at all from the backseat.

"Did you play soccer today?"

"It's hard," Jeremy concedes after we've driven another several miles or so, after rural has become suburban, and we've left the country road and joined up with the highway. "Soccer's hard," he says again, and it's clear that that is all he can bear to tell me. I don't know what happened at recess. I don't know whether my son played and got pushed, or played and grew confused, or didn't get to play at all. But it's definite that something's happened and just as definite that it would hurt to explain, and I don't want to deepen his wound, so I do not force a confession.

"I know," I tell Jeremy. Inadequate words, and all that I have. "Soccer is hard. I believe you."

But soccer's hardness, this much is true, will neither dissuade nor diminish my son. For at Jeremy's core is a rich web of fibers; it's pure persistence inside, the odds-smashing stuff of stars and star light. I respect and I celebrate the stubborn, awesome bone of him, the valor that knocks flat whatsoever inconveniently rises up, the strictures that throw themselves against his soul. When Jeremy was two, three, four, when he was five, obtuseness pressed in from every side. Words, for example, were bewildering to him, hard to assimilate, wring free of meaning, and mete out. Society itself was an underwater country—disturbing and irritating, offering few ports of entry. Spoons, tricycles, crayons, swings, balls—easy for other children, but infuriatingly difficult for Jeremy, diagnosed as he was with an autism spectrum disorder. Entanglements and setbacks and deep-seated frustrations were the stuff of Jeremy's childhood. The offices of therapists. The dismal predictions of so-called experts. Only one person, in the end, could expel the label, dispel the myth, repel the very notion that my only child was to live life at its margins. It was Jeremy, and only Jeremy, who masterminded his own survival.

So now Jeremy is eight, and he has friends, and he is academically sound, and he is my hero, make no mistake about that. But he's also my little boy, and I'd fight a den of lions on his behalf, defend his honor to the galaxy's end, hurl myself between him and any alien life force. Survival instincts, in mothers, always suggest themselves first, so that my first sorry inclination, when soccer starts troubling him so, is to tease him away from his newest passion. It seems the smartest, kindest thing to do, given the hurdles that remain. Impaired response time. Poor muscle tone. Limited spatial perception. No team experience. No experience with complex strategies. Besides, flowers full tilt with their blooms aren't as gentle as the child now inexplicably enamored with a sport that requires hustle, aggression, warrior tactics. "I really love soccer," Jeremy's saying, now that we're home. After a Popsicle and graham crackers, he says it again: "Soccer is the game that I love."

It's a good thing that we have a ball. It's a good thing that we have a backyard and two splintered, goal-like sawhorses and sneakers for the both of us. Out we go, and we start to practice, and since I'm deficient in soccer scholarship, our first home-front practice consists of tapping the ball meagerly to and fro. We stand close enough to each other to accommodate the modest momentum we drum up, and Jeremy squints when the ball comes his way, readies his feet, lifts his leg, aims, smacks the grass blades with the soles of his rubber shoes. The ball skips past him, over the crinkle of fallen maple leaves. Retrieving it, he taps it my way, and I lunge at his scattershots, nudge them right back to him, deploy my best coach-like repartee. The afternoon spills its shadows across our lawn. It's nippy out here in the near dark. We take a break and I ask Jeremy if he's happy now, if he realizes how many times he touched the ball.

"This doesn't count, Mom." He rolls his eyes. "You don't really count, even though I love you. Touching my foot to the ball only counts when I'm at school."

"Yeah?" I say.

"Yeah," he says. He retreats to his own fantasies.

We need soccer books, and we get them. We need soccer videos; they're acquired, too. We need my husband, slight in frame and still graceful at forty, a Salvadoran by birth, a bit of an expert on soccer. Pretty soon, on the warm-enough nights and weekends, the two of them are out playing the game, and I'm cheering them on from the deck. We buy glowing red cones and string them like Christmas bulbs across the yard. We invite soccer-minded school-mates to play. My husband teaches Jeremy the rules of the game on thick pieces of oversized paper. We are terribly indulgent parents. We do what we can to help our son fan his flame.

Still, school has become an unhappy trial; blanched trails of tears lengthen the verticals of Jeremy's face. Nearly every day now there's a quiver in his lip, a stoicism, an expressed desire to speak of anything but recess. It is only after weeks go by that Jeremy courageously drops his guard: "They make fun of me," he tells me. "Out on recess. When I play." We're in the midst of a dull, warm-weather winter, driving the familiar trek home. I'm aware, all of a sudden, that the sky is rammed against the earth. That the clouds are pressing close, like fog. My own imagination is a dangerous habitat as—rapidly, unstoppably—terrifying images grow crystal clear. Bestial children. Minor criminals.

"What do the kids say, Jeremy?" I ask, after I've already seen the whole awful mess in my mind's eye.

"That I shouldn't play." Jeremy starts to whimper. "That I don't know the rules. And why can't I stay in the sandbox with James and why don't I take some lessons or something, and soccer is for good players, soccer's not for me." Jeremy's words are hardly decipherable. He has started to wail in the back of the car.

"And what do you say, Jeremy?" I manage a civilized question in the quietest possible voice, hoping only, at this moment, to calm him down, make sure he breathes. *I'm going to kill them,* I'm meanwhile thinking. *I'm going to wring their little necks.*

"I say it isn't fair that I'm not any good and it isn't fair that I have to work so hard and it isn't fair that I'm not a hustler because I really love soccer, I really do, and I just want to play, just want to kick the ball once in a game, see what it feels like. I want to play." His words missile at me through a hailstorm of tears. Jeremy pounds his knotted-up fist against the plush taupe cushions of the car.

"Oh, Jeremy." I wish I would reach for him right now, bring the end to his sobbing. We're off the country roads, another five miles from home.

"And they say I'm stupid because I pick up the ball and you can't pick up the ball when you're playing soccer. That's the rules." Jeremy lets the whole story out now, it can't be stopped. His voice gets angrier and louder. His tears fall hard.

"You pick up the ball?" I manage to grab on to a piece of what he's saying, despite my desire, at this moment, to blame the whole damned world for his sorrow.

"I pick up the ball," he says, defiant. "I pick it up. I have to, Mom."

"But why, Jeremy, if it's against the rules? If it's going to get the kids mad, why do you do it?"

"Because how else am I going to get a chance at kicking if they won't let me close and I want to play soccer? I can't keep up. I can't hustle. I have to pick the ball up if I'm going to kick it, and I have to kick the ball, Mom. I have to practice."

More books, more afternoon practice sessions, more studied videos. More recess tears, more profane stories, a burst of truncated tales about show-and-tell soccer trophies. Too many drives home from school that leave us both with a bruise on our hearts, and I start to understand, as with all things Jeremy, that soccer is no longer a sport in our lives; it has become a metaphor. It's the key to another world, an access pass, and we realize, implicitly, that if Jeremy can learn this game, if he can master just one or two of its requisite skills, if someone will give him a chance—goddamn it—he will have pushed through yet another essential door. Closer he will have come to that fickle state "normal." No more will he be on the periphery at recess. No more standing on the sidelines cheering his classmates on, bestowing congratulatory smiles when they proudly showcase the latest in their long line of trophies. It is definitely winter now. I haven't been able to find Jeremy a private soccer coach. Recess is a disaster waiting to happen.

But Jeremy is not giving up. He practices every afternoon, studies his soccer books as if preparing for the bar. One day he announces that he's deriddled the problem. "How's that?" I ask. His answer, straightforward: "I'm going to join the real soccer league. The one my friends play on. I'm going to get good that way. Going to get a trophy for me."

I get another of my furious famous mental pictures now—of tricky-footed kids, of crafty coaches, of upset over errors and defeats. I think about drafts, years of experience, uniforms, the not-so-irrelevant fact that we don't live anywhere near, aren't paying taxes to the township that sponsors Jeremy's chosen league.

"Are you sure, Jeremy?"

"Yes."

"Are you ready for that? I hear it's tough."

He rolls his eyes at his poor and unwise mother. "How am I going to get better, Mom, if I don't sign up and play?"

There are some things that money can't buy and friendship delivers with aplomb. Let me say for the record that I'd be nowhere without my friends. Without the couple of ladies who have made my son part of their families, attended to his winding sentences, included him in every extracurricular gig. These ladies who, when I later report our predicament with the very league their sons have played on for years, promise at once to see what they can do. They lean on their husbands. They get me the paperwork. They let me know when secret draft meetings are conducted. After several weeks of holding our breath, it is outwardly and officially done. Jeremy has been given a berth on the league. He is a Shark, a purple-shirt and plastic-shin-guard guy, an up-and-coming Number 3. For different reasons we tremble, Jeremy and me, when we get the call from the league. This is the big time. This is the Big Jeremy Dream Come True. Only one thing is left for him now, and that thing is to get out there and play.

The first practice session is an out-and-out washout; thunderstorms have rivered the fields. The second practice is canceled, on account of the excess of absentees. We're coming up on our first game now, and there's just one planned pre-season practice to go. It's a Wednesday. The sky keeps its distance. The practice field is prairie flat and dry. We're the first to arrive, by a very long shot, and Jeremy rumbles out of the car, his long, elk legs disguised with thick socks and padding, his feet unsteady on the platform of their plastic cleats. He runs to the field, then dribbles the ball up and down, all around, looking up, frequently, to check for signs of his teammates.

Finally, the other Sharks materialize. We see them trundling up toward the field, postures suggesting that nothing much is doing. The parents, too, appear casual, informal, not particularly worried whether their kid will scoop up the soccer ball in the midst of a frustrating moment. Impromptu drills get initiated up and down the field; kids head the ball, knee the ball, dribble it fiercely past their teammates.

Jeremy, meanwhile, skips up and down the sidelines, hopeful and solo as the tail on a kite. *God,* I think. *Oh God have mercy.* And just then the practice coach arrives. Red-haired, whistle-necklaced, impressively muscled and sound, she totes a fisherman's net full of balls, cones, and nylon shirts, then lays it down. She checks her clipboard and she blows her whistle. On cue, the kids turn and race to where she's standing. Jeremy, way out there, continues his skipping across the field. "Jeremy," I call to him. "Rascal! Get over here with your coach!" Overexcited, he fails to hear. I put down my purse, get myself ready to fetch him. "You stay right here," a well-meaning, been-through-this mother tells me. "He's on his own. The coach knows what she's doing." I nod. I agree. I give her credit for her infinite smarts. I pledge that I will not say another word, then promptly turn my back to the field so that I won't be tempted. If I cannot help, coax, urge, or pull, then right now I cannot watch.

The first real soccer game is just three days later. It's unseasonably cold, and I haven't slept a wink, but Jeremy is up before dawn, donning his purple. He's a handsome Number 3, proud as a colt that has mastered its own weak knees, and I have to admit, my heart is swelling with an arrogance all its own. I can't myself get over this. Never, in all these mixed-up, utterly fierce, and emotional years as a mother, did I imagine my boy suited up for a team. "You're the best," I tell him. "You really are." Because no matter what happens in this next hour or so, he's already beaten more miserable odds.

Now, I'm not going to nudge you through every shoelace detail of this first, bewildering game. I'm not going to say how unnerved I feel, how afraid of the opposing team, assailants in blue. I'm not going to say that the field seems vast and the netted goal cages loom large or that I have a bad case of chills by the time the whistle blows. I'm not going to say just how I feel when Jeremy, anointed left wing, trots gamely out to his position, or how I start trotting myself, acutely on edge, up and down, up and down, in the grassy sideline margins.

I'm not going to say much more, in short, than that it's hard, it is breath snatching, it is downright thrilling, this first game. It is Jeremy alive with challenge as I've never seen him before, Jeremy committing every inch of his devoted self to the rules, to the frenzy, to the wild, zagging play. Three times, right at the end, Jeremy taps his foot against the ball. Three times, in a real league game, he plays his part, while my husband screams and I scream and our voices get lost in the wind. Jeremy plays brave, and I hold my own—stay put, where I finally understand that I belong, on the parental side of the narrow white line.

I tell Jeremy, many weeks later, that I am going to write his soccer story. I tell him this after the season of Wednesday practices and Saturday games has run its course, after I've widened our friendships with the other soccer moms and dads and with the coaches, who have given us every fair chance and more to earn our place on a team of purple shirts. I tell him this after the tears have stopped at recess because he's playing now by recess rules, because new friends and two coaches, at least, have taught him how. I tell him this after I have been given the delirious memory of watching Jeremy receive a trophy all his own. Jeremy of the Sharks, it says, a little gold plaque beneath a little gold man. A blazing glory, a shining tribute that now sits on our mantel among our most priceless things.

Jeremy says that it's all right to tell the tale, and then he tells me what plot points to inculcate. "Tell them, first, that I stayed away from the ball because I was afraid of the ball, even though I really love soccer," he instructs. "Tell them that I got better, I improved, that I'm still working on my hustle. Tell them about how we won the first game and tied another, and how we lost the rest, but once it wasn't our fault. That referee had no business calling that game. He was color-blind, couldn't tell the purple shirts from the blues."

"What else?" I ask, eager for more, and he says, "Tell them about the assist, tell them that. Tell them how, in the fifth game, I wasn't afraid anymore, how I took the ball from midfield to the goal. I passed it to Garrett, because Garrett's the best, because I knew that if I got it to Garrett, he would score."

"Don't worry," I tell Jeremy. "That's going in there. That's really key."

"Yeah," Jeremy says. "Yeah. And you can tell them that you and Dad weren't the only ones screaming for me, Mom. Everyone else was too. All those other moms and dads. The coach. They were cheering for me, too. They were cheering like I was important. They were cheering like they cheer for real teams."

"Yeah," I say. "Don't worry. That's sacred. That's in."

"Yeah," Jeremy says. "Yeah. Scoring an assist is a whole lot bigger than getting your foot on the ball." He nods with thorough, disarming intelligence. I get the sense that he's trying to simplify the hard stuff for me.

"Either one," I say, "seems pretty special. And your team—all those Kevins and a Devin... I'm never going to forget them, will you?"

"Yeah. Well. That's pretty much it," Jeremy says, his forehead in a fit of lines as he tries to scrounge up any last relevant details. "I think that's it. Really. That's what you should say."

"Okay," I tell him. "That's plenty for the story I want to tell."

"Yeah. Except maybe? If there's room? You can tell them about professional soccer."

"Professional soccer?" I ask, my pencil hung in midair.

"Yeah," he answers, so full of surprises, next steps, bigger dreams, star-blinding faith. "Professional soccer. Like how I'm going to play it, either when I'm a teen or a grown-up. Or I'll play in the Olympics. Or in the World Cup. I don't know which. But you can tell them, if there's room, that they'll definitely see me on TV."

"Yeah," I say softly, "I'll tell them that. I think I will." Because I'm flung back over that line and right smack in there with my little boy and his big ambitions. I'm on his side. I'm throwing caution to the wind. Because he can do it. He can do anything. Just give him the chance. Call him a Shark. Put him on your team.

When I asked my students to point to specific passages that allowed them to know Beth and Jeremy, one of them said:

After Jeremy tells [his mother] that he and James were digging for China just to dig, she asks, "So then what happened?" followed by the narration "My question: quiet and cautious." Kephart could have left this narration off and gone immediately to Jeremy's response, but instead, in those five words she reveals her tone, which gives us a window into her character. She is a person who slows down enough to let her son reveal himself, even if she is not comfortable with what this might mean. We get the sense that she has been here before, that she knows her son well, that she pays close attention, and also that she knows her question may be opening a can of worms. Yet, she chooses to ask the question anyway. Here is a mother who, despite her fear, is going to meet her son where he's at, deal with whatever he's dealing with, find out what's going on for him. No matter how uncomfortable she is, she is not going to gloss over the nitty-gritty nuances of his day, painful or not. She is scared, yes (quiet and cautious), but she is also brave (she does in fact ask the question).

About Jeremy, this student said:

> After he and his mom are kicking the soccer ball and she asks if he realizes how many times he's touched it, he says, "This doesn't count, Mom." He rolls his eyes. "You don't really count, even though I love you. Touching my foot to the ball only counts when I'm at school." Telling his mom that this doesn't count tells us that he means business about this soccer; he's no longer at an age at which he considers "winning" with his mom to be enough. That he says, "even though I love you," tells us that he is sensitive to her feelings. He is not one to necessarily take his frustrations out on her. To me, this speaks of a maturity that makes me think there is a lot to this young person, that there are deep and nuanced complexities to his character. As difficult as things like soccer have been for him, here he is thoughtful beyond his years. It shows that his developmental issues do not limit him across the board, do not define every single aspect of his character.

Kephart shows us her son in scene: We see him sitting in the backseat crying. We see him racing up and down the soccer field during his first practice, overexcited. And we see him triumphant at the end of the essay. But Kephart also uses backstory and summary to help us know and understand her son: We learn that he has an autism spectrum disorder. We learn about his "impaired response time. Poor muscle tone. Limited spatial perception. No team experience." These are things about him that she summarizes quickly to give us context.

Another student raised an interesting point about how little Kephart mentions her husband in this essay. We know he's from El Salvador and that he loves soccer and is a dedicated father, but we don't really "see" him here. I think she probably keeps him on the sidelines (no pun intended) because he doesn't play a crucial role in this piece. In Kephart's wonderful memoir *A Slant of Sun*, which is about discovering and navigating Jeremy's early diagnosis with the autism spectrum disorder, her husband is very present. (I'll include a short excerpt from that memoir in Chapter 10: Our Parenting Partners.) And in her subsequent memoir, *Still Love in Strange Places*, her husband is the main character. You should look at what role your spouse/children/parents play in a scene or situation and go from there. Ask these questions: Do you need them there? Do they need to be fleshed out or will a few lines of description do?

Now I want to turn to a short piece by Sara Martin. Sara uses physical descriptions of her son, Toby, in "Music in His Genes" to give us a sense of who he is. How else do we get to know Toby and Sara in the following piece?

Music in His Genes

My son, Toby, stops mid-gait in the center of our sunny living room and begins to bounce up and down to "Birdhouse in Your Soul," by They Might Be Giants. He looks around to make sure the members of his audience—me, his dad, Tim, and our dog, Harvey—are paying attention; that he is the center of our universe. Toby stomps his feet for emphasis and shakes his head back and forth to the beat until he falls to the floor in a dizzy fit of laughter. At 21 months, he craves the comfort of music the way other kids his age rely on their blankets.

Toby claps his hands for Bach, screams "yeah!" for Johnny Cash, and closes his eyes and rocks back and forth to John Coltrane. He first noticed the television when Eminem grooved to "Lose Yourself" in an iPod commercial. Whenever the speakers in our house fall silent, Toby emphatically points at the stereo.

Tim and I are not particularly musical. Before Toby came home, our car radios were permanently tuned to Minnesota Public Radio news, and our stereo might sit silent for days. Now, music accompanies all of our daily activities; we eat dinner, sweep the floor, and brush our teeth to a beat.

I think of my son's imagination as a continuous "Stomp" performance. He is as likely to find music in the gentle lapping of water on the rocks surrounding a lake as in the "thunk...gshhh...clank" heard at a construction site. From Toby, we've learned that music follows us everywhere.

When parents get together, the conversation often turns to the sources of their children's traits—the dimple in a chin or a love of books. But it's different when a child joins a family through adoption. When I see Toby bouncing along to whatever happens to be coming from our stereo, I wonder about his birth parents. We don't know much about them, except that they made the difficult decision to place Toby for adoption.

Toby's intense love of music makes me wonder whether he was surrounded by music before he was born. Did his birth mother sing lullabies to him in utero? Maybe she played the violin, or liked loud Korean pop. Did Toby's paternal grandfather play the janggu, an hourglass-shaped drum? Or maybe his maternal great-grandmother plucked a gayageum, a traditional Korean instrument.

Although we'll probably never know exactly where Toby's love of music came from, I know it did not start with us. His foster mother, Mrs. Kim, who cared for him for more than seven months, said he always loved music. By the time he was nine months old, he'd developed a preference for a certain collection of Korean children's songs. Mrs. Kim gave us the CD, and it provided a comforting link to his past while Toby adjusted to life with us.

I know this won't be the last time one of his obsessions takes over our home. And it won't be the last time I wonder where it came from. We know we will never be able to firmly tie his traits to either nature or nurture, but if Toby masters molecular physics, we'll thank his birth family profusely. He won't get that from us any more than he got his gorgeous black hair from our Scandinavian gene pool.

For now, back in our living room, Toby is satisfied that he has our attention. He smiles, giggles, and turns to face the magical source of this thing called "music." He holds his arms straight out to the sides for balance, and he bounces, just off the rhythm, knees bending deep, with his diaper-padded bottom sticking out as a counterweight to his head. And the beat goes on.

Martin begins her piece by describing her son doing the thing that he loves most: "Toby stomps his feet for emphasis and shakes his head back and forth to the beat until he falls to the floor in a dizzy fit of laughter." We all have the things that we love to do, things that feel most natural to us. One way to allow readers into the characters of your children is by painting a picture of them "in their element," doing the things they love to do.

In this piece, Martin also gives us a quick sense of who she and her husband are with this summary paragraph: "Tim and I are not particularly musical. Before Toby came home, our car radios were permanently tuned to Minnesota Public Radio news, and our stereo might sit silent for days. Now, music accompanies all of our daily activities; we eat dinner, sweep the floor, and brush our teeth to a beat." And later, she lets us know that Toby was adopted from Korea, and that she wonders about his birth parents.

As I mentioned at the beginning of this chapter, when you write your children, *you* get to decide how the reader first sees them. Both Kephart and Martin wait to tell us certain details about their sons. Kephart doesn't mention that Jeremy has an autism spectrum disorder until we've "seen and heard" him, until we've come to know him a little. Similarly, Martin does not tell us that Toby was adopted until halfway through "Music in His Genes." This is important because so often if we know that someone is different, whether it's because this person has a disability or was adopted, we attach a whole set of expectations and stereotypes to him or her, and this gets in the way of actually seeing the person there; we end up only seeing the difference. I'm sure if you are living with a disability or have a child with a disability, you are all too familiar with this scenario. But when you write about your children, you can wait to describe a wheelchair or mention that your skin colors are not the same until after the reader is already invested in your child. That is a wonderful thing.

Character is something we'll come back to again and again, but think about how character is revealed as you read the essays and poems in the following chapters.

WRITING EXERCISE:
IN HER ELEMENT

With Sara Martin's "Music in his Genes" in mind, try to describe your child or children "in their element." What is the activity you most closely associate with them? What is the thing they love to do most of all? Describe them doing this thing. Use as many concrete, sensory details as possible to create a scene.

WRITING EXERCISE:
CELEBRATE AND ADMIRE

In "The Line is White and It is Narrow," Beth Kephart writes, "I celebrate the stubborn, awesome bone of him, the valor that knocks flat whatsoever inconveniently rises up, the strictures that throw themselves against his soul." What are the characteristics of your child that you most celebrate and admire? Why? How are you different or similar?

WRITING EXERCISE:
CHARACTER SKETCH

This is one of my favorite exercises because it allows me to stop and describe one of my daughters in as much detail as possible. Whether or not what you're writing develops into something longer, you'll always have this sketch to return to.

Think of your child (or one of your children if you have more than one). Try to convey his personality by using dialogue, gestures, and facial features. Ground your writing in detail. It may help to think in terms of objects—what your child eats, what he likes to play with, his hobbies. What does her face look like when she is absorbed in a task? Write as if you are watching your child from the other room. What does she look like when she doesn't realize that you're watching?

Writing babies can sometimes be challenging because they don't *do* that much. So if you have a very small baby, you might choose to describe her while she's sleeping, or crying, or gnawing on her hand. Or you can try this exercise with another person in your life.

Note: Some of my students who have twins have found that they cannot write about one without writing about the other. If you have multiples and feel this way, go ahead and write them together in a scene. Think in terms of differences and similarities. When are they most alike, most different?

CHAPTER 5

VOICE IN
CREATIVE NONFICTION

WHEN I BEGAN WRITING, I COULDN'T GET MY MIND around the concept of voice. Everyone seemed to be talking about "finding" their voices, and I was frustrated because I wasn't sure I had one. And I wasn't sure how to get one.

I didn't think I had much say when it came to voice. I thought that while it was possible—and necessary—for fiction writers and poets to craft voice in order to meet the needs of specific characters, nonfiction writers were left with only their *own* voices, the ones we use in daily life.

But in *The Situation and the Story*, Vivian Gornick discusses the need of a successful nonfiction writer to pull from one's own self the narrator who can tell the story that needs to be told—a narrator with a unique voice. She describes her struggle to find the right tone of voice in which to write her memoir *Fierce Attachments*. She realized that her ordinary, everyday voice wouldn't work. When she finally settled on a voice that was controlled enough to deal with the subject matter—her relationship with her mother—she realized she had created what she calls a persona. This persona was the part of her that "could not leave her mother because she had become her mother," the part that needed to tell that specific story.

Gornick's persona, to me, is a combination of voice and character. It is the feel, language, tone, and syntax that makes a writer's writing unique. In nonfiction, voice is you, but not necessarily the you sitting in front of your computer typing away. Voice can be molded by a writer to serve the subject about which she is writing.

Sometimes the writing comes out in a voice that serves the needs of your piece. But sometimes you need to look at sentences and really craft a voice that works for your subject matter. Sonya Huber, author of *Opa Nobody* and *Cover Me: A Health Insurance Memoir*, describes the challenge she had in settling on the voice for *Cover Me*:

> I've been so angry for so long about the state of healthcare access in this country that the first years of writing were, to put it politely, pure spew. And I didn't want to assault the reader with that—I wanted to bring something to the reader. This ended up being a problem of voice. I had to work to make the material approach-able and funny, to connect it to a situation that makes me angry while at the same time allowing for breaks and distance.

Sometimes it takes time to settle on the right voice to tell your story. When I began writing my memoir, I was so worried that the book would sound sentimental—*My baby! Oh my baby!*—that I was holding back, and as a result my voice came across as very distant. Early readers commented that they weren't getting a sense of me as a character. It was only after several drafts and hundreds of pages that I felt I was myself on the page, letting my in-the-moment reactions and emotions seep into the prose and also letting in the parts of me that are some-times funny, irreverent, and neurotic. This allowed me to settle on a voice that feels authentically mine and is also, I hope, accessible to readers.

Sonya Huber described doing a recent reading of excerpts from both her memoirs, *Opa Nobody* and *Cover Me*. She said, "I was really shocked at how different the voices are. That made me happy because it's something I tell my students, and it's actually been borne out in practice: that the voice fits the subject matter and leads to the approach for the book."

So voice can change from book to book, depending on the needs of your subject, and it changes as we grow and change as people. If you write about a situation today and again in 10 years, your take on it will probably be different, and so will your voice.

But you also can employ different voices in one piece of writing. As mothers, think of this as inhabiting your different identities—mom, woman, daughter, sister, friend, professional. How do these identities sound and feel different? How does your voice change as you shift from one identity to another?

In her wonderful writing book *Fearless Confessions: A Writer's Guide to Memoir*, memoirist Sue William Silverman describes the different voices that can work in one piece of creative nonfiction:

My observation, both from writing and reading essays and memoirs, is that most writers employ two major voices in their work. I've defined these voices by re-imagining phrases originated by William Blake, labeling one a Song (or Voice) of Innocence, the other, a Song (or Voice) of Experience.

The Song (or Voice) of Innocence relates the facts of the experience, the surface subject. It's the voice that, in effect, says, "first this happened, then this happened, and then this happened." It reveals the sequence of events, the particulars of your experience, whether in a one-page essay or a full-length book. It's the innocent "you"—who you were when the events actually occurred. In my memoir *Because I Remember Terror, Father, I Remember You,* for example, this voice is characterized as the little girl "me" who is being sexually molested by my father. Because this voice is confused and scared, I/she only knows enough to relate the facts of what happened.

The Voice of Experience is then twined to this Voice of Innocence, thus adding a more mature author persona. This second narrator establishes the progression of thought in creative nonfiction, allowing the reader to know what the Voice of Innocence, what the facts, mean. By use of irony and metaphor, it interprets the surface subject. This voice, in effect, reflects back on the story, the past, and guides the reader through the maze of the experience. In *Terror, Father,* a simplified example of a Voice-of-Experience sentence could be: "Because my father misloved me, I had no sense of my true self growing up, no language to understand what happened to me." This reflective narrator would then proceed to develop this idea of identity and language into a metaphor and theme for the entire memoir.

In my second memoir, *Love Sick: One Woman's Journey Through Sexual Addiction,* I implement an addict voice (the Song of Innocence) and a sober voice (the Song of Experience). Here is an example that utilizes both voices, where I, a college freshman, describe my feelings toward a scarf given to me by my older, married lover: "I press the scarf against my nose and mouth. I take a deep breath. The scent is of him—leaves smoldering in autumn dusk—and I believe it is a scent I have always craved, one I will always want. I don't understand why the scent of the scarf ... seems more knowable, more tangible than the rest of him."

Here, I begin in the addict persona where the Voice of Innocence romanticizes the man and the maroon-scarf scent before moving into a more sober persona, the Voice of Experience, which reveals that the scarf is a metaphor for alienation, loneliness, loss. This sober, experienced voice, in other words, guides the reader through the quagmire of the addiction.

The "then" voice (or self) in creative nonfiction is the one experiencing the events in the past. The "now" self is the one who is writing, thinking about thoughts and events and reflecting on what has happened. This reflective narrator is what Silverman calls the "Voice of Experience" above. Because we are striving to move beyond "this happened and this happened," we need our "now," reflective voice also to be present on the page, making connections and making sense of what we have experienced.

Read the following excerpt from Jill Christman's "The Allergy Diaries" with these different aspects of voice in mind. First, how would you describe Christman's voice in this piece? Who is this narrator? (This is the part of voice that seems slippery—the essence of a writer.)

After you have described her, look for places in her writing where her voice resides. Which sentences help you know her as a narrator? Can you note the areas where she is more reflective versus more in-the-story? How do these different voices work together?

The Allergy Diaries

. . . .

Months before my first baby was born here in the middle of Indiana, I received an invitation from a university in Alabama to give a reading, and having no real idea what it means to leave a breast-fed four-month-old baby, and imagining in my gestational brain this liquid marriage between my writer/teacher life and motherhood, I accepted the invitation. Go ahead and chuckle.

So a good two months before my scheduled trip, I started to panic. I wanted my husband, Mark, to fly down with me and hang out with Ella in the hotel room while I gave the reading, but he had to stay home to teach. Mark is, I suppose it should be said— although it never is, is it?—a *working father*, and he was going to be juggling an infant and three classes all on his own for thirty-six hours. While Mark himself seemed oddly serene, I ratcheted myself up to a skin-prickling level of preparatory fear. How could I leave my baby? But somewhere in Birmingham, Alabama, flyers had been posted with my face on them. Could I call up and say,

You know what? I'm so sorry, but I haven't seen Jill Christman for months. She's going to have to cancel.

Sometimes Mark and I wonder what our lives would be like if I had actually gotten on the plane on that morning in February. How things would be different. And I wonder if my dread—even then, before I knew what I know now, before I'd scratched in additional Things to Fear like items on a grocery list—was common sense trepidation (i.e., any fool knows not to schedule an overnight journey with a four-month-old exclusively breast-fed baby) or a kind of misguided presentiment? Was my maternal premonition a genuine thing? Did I *know* something was going to go wrong? The answer to this question matters, of course, and I will never know the answer. Of course.

In the preceding weeks, I pumped like a madwoman, throwing back the black leather flap that dressed up the electric milking machine, this dairy barn in a bag, as a hip briefcase, and submitting to the only aspect of motherhood I truly loathe. Wedged between the counter and the refrigerator with my breasts suctioned into their respective funnels, I tried not to despair as I watched one mean droplet at a time trickle down the plastic tubing and into the waiting bottles. I hooked myself up three times a day and froze the milk flat in special breast milk bags, but even so, the supply was meager. I hoarded that stuff like Gatorade in a fall-out shelter. "Listen," I'd say to Mark as I sprinted out the door to teach, "I'll be home at five. If you can hold her off, hold her off, okay?" Poor kid.

So we arrived at the Sunday before my Wednesday journey and I counted the thin, stacked packages of life-giving, scream-stopping milk with the tip of my finger: thirty-six ounces. I had shortened the trip to thirty-six hours, but would one ounce per hour be enough? Lacking easy-to-read calibrations on my breasts, I hadn't the foggiest idea how much milk Ella consumed in a day or how much she'd need while I was gone. We didn't know if we had enough. We knew there was a chance Mark would run out of the frozen bags and be forced to peel open a can of formula.

That's why we did what we did, but I cannot tell you why we decided that seven p.m. on a Sunday evening was a good time to find out how well Ella would tolerate formula. We had nearly a case of the stuff stockpiled in the pantry because the formula companies had been sending it to us like sample packs of crack cocaine. The formula would arrive with shiny pamphlets about how "breast is best," but wonder of wonders, if all else failed, the formula would be there, fortified with DHA and ready to replicate nature herself. Here's what we wanted to know: Would she drink it? Would she get gas? Would it make her cranky? We didn't consider the possibility that it could kill her.

So on February 29th—that bissextile window of opportunity that comes around only once every four years—it was my turn to succumb to the formula temptation. I hadn't pumped enough. I was a nervous wreck, my head full of images of my baby screaming in desperate hunger and my equally desperate husband scrabbling through peas and pork chops praying for one more fallen bag of frozen milk. We had to try the formula. Just in case. I was typing up some class prep, pulled up to the table in the dim dining room with Ella resting in my lap on the Boppy pillow. She woke up hungry, and I was ready to breast-feed when I realized this was a good opportunity. "We need to practice with the formula. We could do it now."

Earlier, Mark had made a too-grim-to-be-funny comment that had been intended as a kind of hapless father joke, but turned out to be prescient: "I'd die if she had a reaction to the formula and you weren't here to help. I'd just lie down on the floor and die. And then she'd die too."

"Honey," I'd said, "you would not. You'd get her to the hospital."

"I'd die," he repeated dramatically.

"You would not!" I started to panic. "You would not! You would take her to the hospital!"

"Jill," he said, "I'm kidding. I'm just joking. We're going to be fine. I'm going to take good care of her. You need to *relax*. If we lose our sense of humor, we're sunk, remember?"

And then we forgot all about this conversation until I suggested at seven p.m. that we should give it a try. Mark followed the directions on the can of Enfamil with Iron and filled a bottle. I didn't watch him mix it. He handed me the bottle and I put the nipple between Ella's little lips and she started to suck. She kept sucking.

"She likes it," I reported happily. "Excellent. She likes it!"

My fear had been that she might reject it. I am full of fear. But I never get it right. I am never afraid of the right thing.

Formula leaked down Ella's chin and into the fold of her neck. She stopped sucking and I removed the bottle from her mouth and checked the side—she'd only taken an ounce, but I figured that was good enough for our little experiment. Besides, I needed to finish typing the notes and I couldn't hold the bottle and type at the same time. Sunday afternoon's blue gloom had turned to black and the only light in the dining room was seeping in through the kitchen door. I couldn't see Ella's face. She was in shadow.

"Could you take her and change her diaper?" I called out to Mark. "I just need one more minute."

There must have been several seconds after I handed her off before Mark screamed. "What's wrong with her face? She's getting a rash!" I was up and moving toward Mark and the baby and the rash and then the next ten minutes are panic and screaming and running. On the well-lighted pad of the changing table, I could see the red circle around Ella's mouth, a ring of blistery welts; and even in the seconds I stood there, the welts multiplied and spread, onto her cheeks and down onto her neck, as if we were watching an accelerated film. *We need to wash it off! We need to wash it off!* And I was swabbing a cool, wet cloth over her face and neck, but nothing, and then she started to cry, from watching us, or from her own sense of something terribly wrong, we'll never know, but the cry sounded strangled, as if she were strangling, and that's when the gurgling began—a clog in the drain of the too-small throat of our baby.

The next minutes are a blur. Mark picks her up and runs. I turn circles around the house for seconds that seem like hours—time is all fucked up when your baby is gurgling. I scream that we need to call someone. We need to call the doctor. We need someone to tell us what to do. But Mark has Ella in her car seat and somehow the dogs are locked safely in the house and I am beside Ella in the backseat, leaning over her, listening to the gurgle, watching her face, *come on baby come on baby come on baby*, and Mark is backing up fast.

This is the moment I come back into my mind. There's nobody to call or to talk to—we just need to get to the hospital, and what is so miraculous about this moment is that we live only four blocks from the door of the emergency room. Only four blessed blocks. Ella's not crying anymore. I wish she would cry: red and swollen and gurgling. *Come on baby come on baby come on baby.* And Mark is yelling from the front *Is she okay? Is she okay? Is she breathing? Is she okay?* And that fast we're swinging into the half circle in front of the emergency room doors and I'm unclicking the seat and running with it inside while Mark drops off the car. I have the car seat with my baby's face in sight snug on my hip and I'm running through the revolving door even though I'm claustrophobic and I hate revolving doors because that trapping door is the fastest way to the nurse at the long shiny desk at the back of the waiting room. I see only the face of this nurse, a man, because I know he's my way in. All of the other people in the waiting room look like wallpaper, their faces blending together in a smear of color and expression.

"My baby!" I scream. "My baby's not breathing!" Even in this moment of terror, I know what I am saying is not technically true. She is gurgling. I can hear the sound of air moving in her throat, passing through liquid or swelling or something, but I know that it is there. I do not know how long she will be like this. I do not know how fast this is all happening, and I have never known a more appropriate time for some high-volume hyperbole.

It works. Another nurse appears from behind the first one and runs to the front of the desk. She grabs the handle of the car seat and disappears with my baby through the flapping doors of the ER. There are no insurance forms to fill out. I print Ella's name and sign my own. That is all. "You can follow her," the male nurse tells me. I scream again. "My husband is right behind me. Tell him where we are." Flapping doors have never looked so much like a giant's mouth, a monster's slathering maw, and my baby has gone into them. Inside the doors, people buzz everywhere and my head is whipping, scanning. I feel animalistic, as if I'll smell my baby. That is how I'll find her. At the center of this hive, I see a cluster of people gathered around something on the floor and then I see her foot. Ella is on the floor of the nurses' station and they're drawing up shots.

"How much does she weigh?" someone yells at me, but it's been over a month since her last appointment, and I know she's grown.

I tell them this. "Maybe sixteen pounds."

The infant scale in the ER isn't working and the nurse is screaming. She is panicking. Now Mark is here too. I jump onto the regular scale and yell out the weight. Then I grab Ella and jump on. "Subtract! Subtract!" I shout because I cannot think. I cannot take 162 from 178. Numbers mean nothing. Give her the goddamn shot!

"Sixteen!" Mark shouts. "Sixteen!"

And right there on the floor, the doctor plunges a shot of Benadryl into one thigh and a shot of steroids into the other. The needles look huge. Each one is as long as her thigh itself. When you're a baby in an ER, the proportions are all wrong. Everything is way too big. She is in my arms, wearing only a diaper, and her eyes roll back in her head and then close. "What's happening?

What's happening?" I scream. I think she has died. I think they have killed my baby. The doctor smiles at me. "She's sleeping," he says. "It's the Benadryl. It puts them right to sleep."

All of the ER rooms were full and so we stayed there on the gurney in the middle of all the activity. This was fine with me because when the doohickey that measures the concentration of oxygen in Ella's blood started to beep and the number blinked and descended: 98, 92, 86, 65, 86... I yelled and somebody checked it. The wire had tangled. The clamp on her toe had loosened. It's always something. Ella woke up and I offered her my nipple for comfort. Soon, an older woman—a volunteer?—was throwing a hospital sheet over me and the baby, shielding us as if I had begun a striptease right there in the ER. *Oh we're so sorry*, she mumbled. *For your privacy, for your privacy...*

"I'm fine," I insisted. "I'm okay. Listen, any scrap of modesty I might have had, I lost during childbirth. I don't care."

She continued tucking the sheet around me, trying to hide my breast. "I'm so sorry. We haven't had somebody out here since the new emergency room opened. Every room is full! Here you go."

"Really," I said, fighting an urge to peel my shirt off completely and do a little dance around the emergency room to assert my rights as a nursing mother in a hospital of all places. "I'm really fine." The whole scene felt so otherworldly to me. First, there had been the panic of the reaction—*She could have died*, I kept muttering to Mark, *she could have died. My God. Thank God. You were great. You just ran with her. You were great. Thank God. Oh my God, what if we'd bought the house out in the country? Thank god we live just four blocks from the hospital. She could have died*— the period of calm after the first rush of trauma is not a time of ambitious language. All of my synapses were still swimming in the adrenaline of the moment and I could feel the runoff of the chemicals in my bloodstream, the pollutants circulating down my arms and legs, making my hands and feet feel tingly and not quite a part of me. The only part of my body that felt real and solid was my breast and the small electric pull of Ella's mouth on my nipple, connecting me to her and her to me. I was so grateful to be able to comfort her. Mark and I looked down at our resting baby, breathing fine now, and the beeping numbers of the monitor, assuring us that the oxygen was getting in. The room buzzed around us and Ella started to whimper. I threw the sheet over our heads and made a tent for the two of us, rocking and rocking, singing *Summertime, and the living is easy, catfish are jumpin'...*

Through the filtered light of our white world, I saw the rash spread farther down her naked belly and move onto her thighs. I threw back the sheet and sounded the alarm. The bald-headed doctor was back and ordering an IV. His fear was that Ella could be experiencing a secondary reaction. There was a room for us and we were rushed into it and a team came down from Pediatrics to put in the IV. I remembered one of the nurses as the one who had successfully drawn blood from a feverish Ella two months earlier after her Attila the Hun partner had failed, and I was glad, but when I saw her finger come to rest on Ella's head, palpating the tiny trace of a blue vein running out toward her temple, I felt my knees start to give. "I'm sorry, honey," I said to Ella. "Your daddy's going to stay with you..." And I moved into the hall, to wait and to pray.

In the world outside our own, another family's drama was unfolding. Another baby, a tiny one, only two months old, was turning blue in her struggle to get air. I overheard that her oxygen number had dropped down into the eighties. We two mothers, out in the hall, eyed each other warily. *Come on, little baby*, I thought. *Come on.* A nurse ran into the room with Ella, who was now screaming and screaming and screaming, and I heard her tell our nurse that the little baby needed an IV, her numbers were dropping, and I said, "Go, go...Go help her." What we were doing was a precaution. That baby was fighting for her life. I can't imagine that what I had to say had anything to do with hospital policy, but strangely, it seemed to. One of the technicians went to the other baby. I saw the mother talking to the father in panicked whispers out in the hall. He handed her a pack of cigarettes from the pocket of his jeans. She fled out the front doors with a crazy look in her eyes. Later, we heard the helicopter on the roof and our nurse told us they'd come for that baby. RSV. Respiratory syncytial virus. They were taking her to Indy. *Come on, little baby*, I thought again, *Come on.*

At eleven o'clock, when they brought us up to our room in Pediatrics, I nursed Ella, all wires and toe clamps and beeping monitors, in the vinyl easy chair, as uneasy as such chairs get, and watched the tail end of the Academy Awards, shaking my head at the strangeness of it all and knowing that there would be no reading in Alabama. I would be going nowhere. Mark went home to check on the dogs and brought me back a sandwich. I convinced him to go back and get some sleep and then I considered my options: the uneasy chair or the hospital crib. There was no way I was going to put Ella in the monkey cage of that white metal barred crib alone, so I lifted her little body over the side and then I climbed in myself, curling my big body around hers, and still singing *Your daddy's rich and your mama's good lookin,' so hush little baby, do-on't you cry....* We actually got some sleep, me and my breathing baby.

In the months following this first reaction, when somebody's mother or another suggested that we give some rice cereal, or peas, or bananas a try, I parroted back the doctor's orders that we give her *nothing* but breast milk until she'd been fully tested at six months: *The doctor told us to breast-feed exclusively until after the skin tests. She could die.* My dire warnings never really stuck and I repeated the doctor's orders many times—it's so hard to imagine healthy foods as lethal agents, isn't it? Before that night with the formula, food allergies were not part of my world. Sure, I'd heard stories about kids who were allergic to peanuts—information I stored in the inchoate place in my brain where I'd locked in my only other brush with an epinephrine injection: At a Connecticut cookout when I was maybe six, there was a kid named Tony, a Fresh Air kid from the Bronx who stayed with this family every summer, friends of my dad's. We'd finished husking this giant vat of corn on the cob and we were playing ball on the edge of the yard while the adults dealt with things that weren't a six-year-old's concern—the grilling of burgers and collecting of condiments—when Tony was stung by a bee and started to have a reaction with swelling lips and bent-over wheezing. I remember group panic, the giant shot, and then the end of the party when Tony and our hosts left for the nearest emergency room.

What sticks with me is my horror at what I learned that day: Tony could have died. A bee, a little bee, could kill you. (A bee didn't kill Tony. A couple of years later he was killed by a gun in a Bronx warehouse. The story I heard was that the shooting was accidental. He and some other kids were playing with the gun and it went off.)

Now that I'm writing this, I wonder: was it Tony who had the venom reaction at the barbeque or was it his Connecticut brother? Maybe if I called my father he could tell me which boy it was, but here is the information mashed together in my mother-brain—things that can kill your kid: bees, guns.

Next to this, I add: food.

This essay goes on to describe visits to the allergist, and ends with Christman wondering whether in this case her worrying matters. (Know that as I'm writing this Ella is a happy and healthy seven–year-old who happens to be allergic to milk, eggs, and peanuts.)

Christman's voice is funny and self-deprecating. (This is clear from sentences like, "Go ahead and chuckle" and "We had nearly a case of the stuff stockpiled in the pantry because the formula companies had been sending it to us like sample packs of crack cocaine.") She's also a worrier, which she lets us know throughout the piece. This self-deprecation, humor, and neurosis infuse the piece with a sense of Christman as a character, as a persona.

But Christman's voice also shifts in this piece to reflect the emotional context of the scenes. When Jill and Mark realize that Ella is having an allergic reaction, note what happens to the length of Jill's sentences: "I was up and moving toward Mark and the baby and the rash and then the next 10 minutes are panic and screaming and running. On the well-lighted pad of the changing table, I could see the red circle around Ella's mouth, a ring of blistery welts; and even in the seconds I stood there, the welts multiplied and spread, onto her cheeks and down onto her neck, as if we were watching an accelerated film." Her sentences become long and run-on, punctuated by short, direct statements: "The next minutes are a blur. Mark picks her up and runs. I turn circles around the house for seconds that seem like hours—time is all fucked up when your baby is gurgling. I scream that we need to call someone. We need to call the doctor. We need someone to tell us what to do." This heightens the sense of confusion and panic in these paragraphs.

The other thing Christman does in this paragraph is to shift into present tense at "The next minutes are a blur." She stays in present tense until the immediate danger is over, shifting back into past tense in the paragraph beginning "All of the ER rooms were full..." Present tense can give writing a sense of immediacy and heighten the sense of urgency.

The rest of the piece is in past tense, with the exception of the moments when Christman inserts her "now," reflective self into the writing. She does this in the third paragraph, with "Sometimes Mark and I wonder..." This is an effective way to foreshadow and also to let us know that this isn't over for her—she continues to think about this event and its ramifications.

WRITING EXERCISE:
REPLICATING EMOTIONAL
CONTEXT WITH VOICE

Being able to shift your voice to match the emotional context of a scene takes practice, and one way to get the feel for doing this is by writing the same scene twice, each time with a different emotion in mind. Choose a vivid memory. The first time you write it as a scene, try writing it with hysteria or desperation or sadness in mind. The second time, try writing it with shock or numbness. You can pick any two emotions, but try to write the same scene—it can be a scene you have tried already—with two different emotions in mind. After you have written it twice, read the two versions. How did the scene change depending on the emotion you were trying to convey? How are they the same? Which version feels truest to you?

WRITING EXERCISE:
REFLECTIVE VOICE VERSUS
IN-THE-SCENE VOICE

We'll spend time in the next few chapters discussing how tense and reflection affect voice and the tension in a piece of writing, but you can start experimenting with these different voices. Using Sue William Silverman's terms, Christman's Voice of Innocence in "The Allergy Diaries" is the one that is panicky when Ella has her allergic reaction. Her Voice of Experience is the one that steps in to give Jill's "now" perspective, the one that says, "The period of calm after the first rush of trauma is not a time of ambitious language."

Write about an experience that has stayed with you from a time when your child was young (or even a time when *you* were young). First, describe the experience, the sequence of events, in your voice of innocence. Then, use your voice of experience to reflect on them. Ask questions: Why do I remember this? Why did I or someone else react the way we did? What does this mean to me now? Asking questions is a good way to get into your reflective voice.

It's always important to feel comfortable with your writing voice. When my memoir was first shopped around in 2007, I was told that there was no market for the book. I was told that my subject matter was too dark, too difficult for readers to handle. And though it was frustrating to hear this kind of response, it wasn't as disheartening as hearing that I could write about the hard parts of motherhood as long as I had a more marketable voice, one that was snarkier, edgier, plain funnier.

I was told by one agent that she wanted the book to sound more like Anne Lamott. One editor responded like this: "We're doing fewer and fewer motherhood memoirs and this one isn't going to work for us. It seems like the very best books for us, where motherhood memoir is concerned, are humor memoirs."

But sometimes motherhood isn't funny. I was writing in a voice that not only felt authentic to me; it was a voice that I felt served the narrative. It would have been a disaster—and dishonest—if I had tried to channel Anne Lamott in my memoir. I love her writing, but it's *her* writing; it's not mine. Remember to be authentic—not only to your subject matter, but to your voice.

CHAPTER 6

USING HUMOR AS A TOOL

AS I MENTIONED IN THE PREVIOUS CHAPTER, motherhood isn't always funny, and I sometimes resent the demand to be funny, especially when writing about parenthood. With that said, using humor in your writing can be a powerful tool—an effective way to communicate feelings and to write about topics that are generally unacceptable in the mainstream. Humor lessens the blow, makes hardships and heartbreak, and of course anger, more palatable.

In later drafts of my memoir, I definitely let my humorous side seep more fully into the writing. I use humor as a pressure reliever—it creates a little breathing room in the narrative and gives the readers (and me) a break from tense and emotionally charged scenes. An injection of humor at the right time can lift the oppressive mood of a piece and help get the reader and author through some dark passages.

And sometimes laughing is the only thing you can do to get through the hard stuff. As one of my students said, "Life in the parenting trenches can be heartfelt and frustrating, but you do survive, and sometimes humor is the best medicine."

In the previous chapter we talked about voice and how voice can shift depending on the subject matter and the needs of a piece of writing. An author's voice is also the driving force in a piece of humor writing. As we saw in "The Allergy Diaries," Christman's humor and self-deprecation infuse the piece and are inextricable from Christman as a character, as a persona.

Memoirist Catherine Newman writes about many facets of parenting and life, from pregnancy to faith to evolution to conjoined twins. Whatever the topic, her writing is always infused with humor. In the following piece, notice how Newman employs humor and sarcasm to write about gender stereotypes:

Pretty Baby

Was that you, sitting behind us at *The Nutcracker on Ice*? Remember? Your kid was tangled up in her own scarf and then weeping over a box of spilled raisins before she peed "one tiny tiny drop" into her tights? But still you could hear our Ben's sharp intake of breath when the skaters all glided out in pairs. You heard his whispery-loud "That's so beautiful!" about their powdered white wigs and spingly-spangly outfits, real pretend snow fluttering around them as they twirled their romantic figure eights. Oh, those fancy Victorian parents in *The Nutcracker*! Those mothers skating around in fitted pink-satin waistcoats and full pink-satin skirts, those fathers just barely distinct in their own cotton-candy waistcoats, although they weren't wearing skirts of course—I mean, it wasn't *Nutcracker on Castro Street*, for God's sake. No, the fathers were sporting the super-manly pink-satin *knickers*. And Ben loved them.

Later, when we were zipping up our jackets in the lobby— after the scuffling soldier mice and the various Freudian dream sequences of hunky toys that may or may not come to life and look like a person's dad, after the Dance of the Sugar Plum Fairy and Ben's baby sister falling asleep in my lap like a thirty-pound sack of sausages—Ben identified "that pink part" as the very best segment of the entire evening.

I was not surprised. Ben is five, and pink has always been his favorite color. Just to be clear, we're not talking *pale* pink—which he will tolerate but has no especial affinity for (it ranks seventh on his list, behind even *teal*)—but "bright pink," or what he sometimes calls "darky pink." When, for instance, I wore my reversible down jacket with the black side out, he thought I was insane. "If I had all that nice darky pink in my coat, I would definitely show it." (He had a point. I reversed it.) His own jacket is silver, but his snow boots are flamingo pink, as is the fraying plastic lei from a midwinter luau. His favorite flowers are pink roses. And his most special outfit—the one he wears only for such extraordinary occasions as a birthday party or the weekly show-and-tell at his preschool— involves a floral-printed t-shirt with fuchsia velour sleeves, and the pants that I myself made (with much saying of the F-word and sewing of my actual hand to the fabric) from the magenta-striped terry cloth that Ben picked out from Jo-Ann Fabrics.

Right about now you're probably sending enthusiastic "You go, boy!" vibes in Ben's direction—and you should be. For one thing, he looks absolutely fabulous. And for another, maybe pink is the new navy blue. After all, P. Diddy swaggers in sweatpants the color of a seashell and Demi Moore ogles her young hotty in his taffy-hued suit. Briefcase-carrying hominids seem to have worn sherbety-pink shirts beneath their ties since the Dawn of Business Attire. And yet the color rules are different for little boys. Is that because we imagine a grown man's gender is already hardened and set, like the steely abdomen of masculinity itself, the threat of pink bouncing off it like so many girly punches? While evidently for budding young manhood—the preschool type—pink must be shunned like gender-bending kryptonite. Like it's some queer wolf in powdery-pale clothing. Pink might *seem* to be a swishy little color—but it's got the strength of entire armies. Why, merely gazing too long at a carnation could prevent your son's very testicles from descending! And forget the actual *wearing* of the color— that could send his Y chromosomes leaping for their lives onto the nearest testosterone-leaking Arnold Schwarzenegger look-alike.

I know this must be true, because I write an online parenting column, and whenever I post a picture of Ben in this or that pink outfit—or with the rolling pink Hello Kitty suitcase he wanted (and got) for his fourth birthday—the message boards fill with enraged, Apocalyptic postings about our family's imminent nullification. "Why is your son wearing pink?" is what people want to know— although they don't tend to ask quite so politely. (And you'd be surprised at how unsatisfactory they find the perfectly logical answer "Because pink is his favorite color.") In my heart of hearts, I know that these are the same people whose children would tease Ben if he didn't look so unequivocally excellent—the same people who vote for lobotomized dimwits and shriek "Your epidermis is showing!" at their coworkers. But really. From the shrillness of their indignation, you'd think we were taking Ben back-to-school shopping at Frederick's of Hollywood instead of Old Navy, which is where we actually go (when we're not at the Salvation Army).

And all I'll say is: *you* try convincing a young child to choose from the racks of boy clothes. Do we really expect boys to thrill to one of those midget salesmen outfits—the tomato-red polo shirts and pleated khaki slacks—or over an oatmeal-colored sweater vest and army-green camouflage sweatpants? Are we genuinely shocked that the girls' section—with its plush bubble-gum everything, its rhinestones and puppies and velvet detailing—calls out to some boys like a pastel siren song? Of course not. But even when nobody says it outright, we know what the critics are thinking: let your son wear pink, and you might as well enroll him in Camp Fire Island. Because pink isn't just nouveau Hollywood-hip and retro neo-preppy golf sweaters. It's still totally Elton John and Village People. It still means taking out a lease in Gayville—with an option to buy.

Yes, nobody likes to come right out and say it (actually, plenty do), but that's what all of this is about. Everyone wants to be sure that, a dozen years from now, our sons will have the right kind of prom date—the *vagina* kind of prom date. Which they surely won't unless we police their color choices a little more rigorously. But here's where I get confused—simple pinheaded bigotry aside. If "pink" and "gay" go together like Froot Loops and Toucan Sam, is pink imagined to be the *effect* of gayness? Or its cause? Because if it's the former—if pink is the mere expression of some extant *essential* gayness—well then, what's the point of worrying about it? It's a *fait accompli,* so pour me a glass of champagne, pop in a Barbara Streisand movie, and let's celebrate. But if it's taken instead to be the cause, then how exactly *does* pink make a boy gay? Does he grow up to be a pink-wearing *adult,* at which point other men—woops!—mistake him for a Victoria's Secret model and hit on him by accident and, well, one thing leads to another, when in Rome, etc.? Or do the color waves actually alter his brain chemistry such that his ideal wife spontaneously becomes Tom Selleck? For one thing: I doubt it. And for another: Great—even if it's not Tom Selleck. I'll be delighted. (Wouldn't you much rather, for instance, that your son be *shacked up with* the Queer-Eye Fab Five than waiting shlubbily for them to come and fix him?)

Or is the worry just that pink will keep Ben from achieving his proper patriarchal birthright? *O masculinity! So natural and true! As teetering and precarious as an ice-fishing house built from fairy wings!* Will Ben's preschool class photo be uncovered one day and threaten his entry into the World Wrestling Federation? Will those pink-threaded boyhood outfits prevent him from registering a firearm or sucking beer out of somebody's ass crack at a fraternity hazing? Will he be clinically incapable of slouching in front of the Super Bowl like an overgrown, chili-fed larva? Or do we just worry that he won't know how to camouflage himself properly as an *imbecile stone* when a lover tries to enter together with him into the world of human feelings? I mean, men are great and everything—my own dearly beloved is a man, for example—but the last time I checked, gender roles didn't seem to be working so well for everyone. Why would we take such good care of something that seems to make so many people—gay and straight, men and women—so unhappy? And why on earth would we start so young?

Or younger. Because even when Ben was a mere wisp of a newborn, boyness seemed to cast its peculiar blue shadow over him. Our best friends had had a baby before us, and Ben wore her hand-me-down onesies and rompers, all of them decorated variously with whimsical fruits and zoo animals. Nothing was frilly or girly or even *pink*, but because these were not typical boy-baby clothes—insofar as they were without the obligatory decals of footballs and bulldozers and naked women—Ben was often mistaken for a girl. Which was fine with us—I mean, it wasn't like we needed him to hop up and carve our Thanksgiving turkey or anything. He was only fifteen seconds old, after all. But people would gush over him—"Oh what a pretty baby! Oh she's gorgeous."—and we would beam and nod until the moment they asked his name, when we would have to confess, "Well, actually, it's Ben." And then his admirer would always fall into fits of apology. "Oh my God! I'm so sorry! I don't know how I missed it! I mean, now that I really look—he's so handsome. So *manly*." Even though little Ben would just be dozing neutrally in the front pack, with his rosebud lips and male-pattern baldness. It wasn't like he was cruising for a fiancé. "Oh that's okay," we always said. "We don't care!"

And we didn't. Or at least not about that. Because we *do* care— so much that it's like an ache at the bottom of my throat—about other things. Like Ben's happiness. His wholeness. We want him to be himself, to do the things he likes—however contradictory these things may be. Like the time he was two, and he toddled into the living room with a beaded pink-and-orange evening bag slung elegantly over his shoulder—then turned it over and dumped out a heap of Matchbox cars, vroomed them around like a maniac. Or the summer he wore the T-shirt our artist-friend Meg made him: a little pink scoop-neck with the word "boy" silk-screened in black. He loves glittery purple eye shadow (which he applies only to the groove between his nose and mouth) and his iridescent strawberry-kiwi Bonne Bell Lipsmacker—and also running around, yelling, with a plastic baseball bat stuck out from between his legs. He loves his stuffed Snow Bear so tenderly that his eyes glisten while he cuddles her—but play the associations game with him, and the prompt "boring" will cause him to spit out the words "baby doll" like so much chewed-up tobacco.

Ben wants to decorate his birthday cake with rose petals and also gummy worms. He covets (and wears) bejeweled hair accessories although his own hair is cut short, and he loves stringing glass beads and setting up elaborate tracks for his trains. His very best friend is a girl, but his second- and third-best friends are both boys. He likes to arrange the pansies and bleeding hearts in his grandmother's flower press. Dinosaurs scare him. He's a fearless climber. He recently told me that he thinks he's a fan of the Red Sox, "But," he admitted, "only because of the word *socks*—not because of how they play that game." He's happy and funny and smart. And he's very kind.

Which may be why, at *The Nutcracker*, after we'd gathered up all our mittens and scarves and Ben was twirling merrily toward the exit in blue racing-stripe sweatpants and a pink shirt with a heart on its sleeve, you leaned over your sleeping daughter and whispered to me, "Your son is lovely." And my eyes filled with tears—I could only smile and nod—because it's true. He is. And it was lovely of you to notice.

Has anyone—a stranger or friend—ever criticized your child or your parenting style in front of you? If so, how did this feel? What would you have wanted to say as a rebuttal? So often, when we are in situations like that, it's difficult to come up with the appropriate comeback when we want it. I usually think of the proper putdown hours later, when it does me little good. But you can always write about it, and in writing about it you can process your pain and anger and also maybe get others to think about what they say before they say it.

By writing about the criticism she has received because Ben adores pink, Newman allows us to see the absurdity in the militant color-coding of children's clothes. She invites us into her life and into her mind as she explores this issue. Newman creates intimacy with the reader in this piece in a couple of ways. First, she peppers parenthetical statements throughout the essay: (He had a point. I reversed it.) (with much saying of the F-word and sewing of my actual hand to the fabric). These can overwhelm a piece if they are used too often, but when they are used sparingly, they increase the conversational tone and intimacy of the writing. And intimacy—this feeling that the author is there, sitting across the table, sharing her experience with you—is an important characteristic of memoir and personal essay.

Newman also increases the intimacy of the piece through her use of direct address at the beginning and end: "Was that you, sitting behind us at The Nutcracker on Ice? Remember?"

One of my students said,

Newman's use of direct address makes the reader complicit in her rejection of gender conformity and homophobia. It assumes that we share her indignation at those who would limit her son's personal expression. Direct address allows her to build a case for her worldview—my son's perfect the way he is; there are lots of different ways to be a man—without setting up an opposition with her reader. She doesn't have to convince the "you" she's talking to; she writes as if she knows that we're on her side.

Newman aligns the reader with her supporters. Think about how this might work in your own writing. Try rewriting a scene or a whole essay, incorporating direct address, and see how it changes the feel and the meaning of your piece.

Newman also uses cultural references to upend stereotypes in "Pretty Baby." She places us in a specific time with her use of pop culture references like P. Diddy, Demi Moore, Elton John, Tom Selleck, and the Village People. She grounds her story—her life—in images and information that we know, to which we can relate. You risk alienating readers by using too many cultural references; if readers aren't familiar with them, they might feel left out. But used sparingly, they can be very effective.

Another master of motherhood humor is Anne Lamott. She never shies away from writing about the hard parts of motherhood, but she always writes about challenging parenting moments with humor. Part of why this is so effective is that Lamott isn't afraid to make fun of herself in her writing. Here are a few short lines from *Operating Instructions*, her best-selling memoir about her son Sam's first year:

He loves rocking in the rocking chair. He loves his pacifier. I tried his pacifier myself a few days ago, sat there sucking on it while I watched TV, and then I threw it down in fear, absolutely convinced, old addict that I am, that I'd get hooked immediately. By the end of the week I'd be abusing it, lying about how often I was using it, hiding it in the hamper [...]

Both Newman and Lamott juxtapose objects and ideas that don't normally go together. Newman connects *The Nutcracker* and Castro Street (San Francisco's major gay neighborhood), and she gives us the image of a baby carving a Thanksgiving turkey. Lamott compares a pacifier to a drug addiction. This is an effective way of highlighting the absurd in certain situations. The following exercise will help you try this in your own writing.

> ### *WRITING EXERCISE:*
> ### *HUMOR AND PAIN, HAND IN HAND*
>
> Humorous writing often arises out of things that are infuriating or disheartening. (Gender is a good topic to start with, because people can be so judgmental and opinionated when it comes to gender expectations.) Think of a time when someone said something about your parenting style or your child that made you angry or sad. Write a scene about it using as many details as possible.
>
> After you have written your scene, make a list of details that could benefit from absurd comparisons such as the ones that Newman and Lamott employ. Jot these comparisons down next to your piece. Once you have a list of them, rewrite your scene, incorporating the comparisons. How does this change the feel of your piece?

SARCASM

Another strategy that both Newman and Lamott employ is sarcasm. Newman writes: "Pink might seem to be a swishy little color—but it's got the strength of entire armies. Why, merely gazing too long at a carnation could prevent your son's very testicles from descending!" Sarcasm can be powerful, but as one of my student's said, "It's important to notice when writing is being funny/sarcastic for the sake of funny/sarcastic, and when writing uses humor and sarcasm as a tool to say something else or dive more deeply into a subject." Sarcasm is another technique that, if used sparingly and with a purpose in mind, can be very effective.

WRITING EXERCISE:
SARCASM AND SENTENCE STRUCTURE

Choose a short piece that you have already written. (It could be your writing from the humor exercise above or something else.) What happens when you rewrite it with sarcasm? What happens when you shorten some of your sentences and make them very direct, like Newman's here: "He had a point. I reversed it."? Play with these two elements—sentence structure and sarcasm. Does employing sarcasm allow you to dive more deeply into your subject?

CHAPTER 7

❧❧❧

MOTHER FEAR

ON AUGUST 1, 2007, THE I-35 BRIDGE SPANNING THE Mississippi River in downtown Minneapolis collapsed, crumpling into the river, killing 13 people and injuring 145. It's the bridge I took to pick up Stella from preschool, a bridge that countless people used to get to and from work each day, and suddenly it was gone, cars and concrete and twisted metal heaped in the river below.

The night after the bridge collapsed, when Stella was safely in bed, I climbed into my own bed, but I couldn't get the bridge and the victims and their families out of my mind. The Twin Cities are divided by a huge river, and in our daily lives we must cross it again and again. I lay in bed thinking about how vulnerable we are and how unpredictable life is, and I could feel my chest tightening. What if I had been on the bridge? What if Stella had been with me? What if we had plunged into the river and I couldn't get her out of her car seat? Out of the car? Safely to shore? I suddenly saw myself struggling to reach her in the dark, cold water. I saw myself not being able to save her. Then I shook my head and told myself, *Stop it. Stella is safe. Take a breath. Breathe.*

But the image of our car in the river, of me reaching for my daughter, had grabbed hold of my mind. I couldn't stop the possibilities, the what-ifs. Finally I got out of bed and went back into Stella's room. Strands of hair stuck to her sweaty face, her mouth open in sleep, her sheets twisted around her legs. My eyes were suddenly full of tears, the fear and danger still in my throat. I climbed into bed next to her and held her sleeping body, kissed her damp, dear face, not wanting to let her go.

Even before I became pregnant, I seemed to have perfected mother fear. I worried that my yet-to-be-conceived children might suffer depression and anxiety as teenagers and young adults, as I had. Or worse: what if they developed schizophrenia, as their paternal grandmother had? I fretted, I worried, I researched, and finally I decided my desire for children outweighed my fear of mental illness. (I say "I" rather than "we" here because Donny wasn't worried about these things. He was ready to take the leap into parenthood months before I was.)

But like Jill Christman in "The Allergy Diaries," it turns out that I was not afraid of the right things. Stella's prematurity knocked me off my feet, and for a while we had a slew of very legitimate things to worry about: Would Stella breathe on her own? Would she suffer brain damage from the ventilator? Would she die from the sepsis she developed in the hospital? Would she get a cold and land back in intensive care after we had finally taken her home? These, of course, were fears based on real dangers that our fragile daughter faced. But many of my mother fears are not. Just the possibility of something happening to one of my girls is enough to make my heart pound.

Some of this is simply the result of being moderately—or very—neurotic. And if I may, I'd like to blame that on *my* dear mother and the dire warnings on which she raised us: *Never hide in an old refrigerator when you're playing hide-and-seek! Always make sure the elevator car is really there before you step through those open doors!* I'd like to point out that neither did we live near a landfill where you might find abandoned refrigerators nor in a tall building that necessitated regular elevator use. (But I love you, Mom!) Some of my fear is probably attributable to the general focus on fear in our culture. (Have you seen the evening news lately?) But some of my mother fear is simply the result of a maternal desire to keep my children safe. I won't argue whether that is a biological or a learned response to motherhood; all I know is that if my girls are in danger, or seem to be, I go into protection and panic mode. It even happens, in the case of the bridge collapse, that just contemplating my children's involvement in a disaster can send me reaching for them.

Even if your fears are not as highly refined as mine, most of us worry about our children. And these worries swirling around in our mother heads can be powerful forces in our lives. We can fret and fret, but in the end, we don't know what (if anything) might happen to our children, which makes keeping them completely safe impossible. Ona Gritz taps into this idea in the following poem:

This

Already, he has fallen head first
off the back of the couch,
held a rusted nail in his mouth
without swallowing it down.
I keep the television black,
newspapers folded on the porch.
Still, the stories find me. Airplanes
fall from the sky with children in them.
A young man hikes into the mountains
and is never found. One night, my son
takes the hand of another four-year-old
and runs across a thoroughfare.
If I'd left him what he was, a thought,
I wouldn't have become this,
a crazy woman whispering thank you
to unseen beings in the air.

How many times since becoming a mother have you felt like a "crazy woman whispering thank you / to unseen beings in the air"? The line "Still, the stories find me" especially resonates with me. Before I had children, I was a huge fan of television hospital dramas, *ER* in particular. But after Stella was born, I could rarely watch a whole episode, and I finally gave it up altogether. Each episode seemed to feature children who were hurt either by an accident or by some kind of abuse, and like Gritz, I didn't have room for that in my head. Shows like that and the evening news are difficult for me to watch because there is no narrator reflecting on the heartbreak, processing the loss; it's just plain heartbreaking.

But writing is different. As I mentioned in Chapter 2, in memoir and personal essay the author is present, struggling for honesty, searching for meaning. I'm drawn to writing about fear and heartbreak (which I'll discuss in more depth in the next chapter) because I'm interested in how different writers and mothers process these emotions. In *Bird by Bird*, Anne Lamott says, "Write straight into the emotional center of things." She advises, "Write toward vulnerability." When you are writing toward the parts of you that are most vulnerable, there will be conflict, and where there is conflict, there is a compelling story.

But writing our fears can also change us as mothers. When I asked my students how writing their mother fears has affected them, one of my former students responded:

Writing my fears helps to "deflate" them; I get them out of me and onto the paper, where they have less dimension. I can read them and reread them, and because I am reading them now with the eyes of a writer instead of a scared mother, they have less power. I can reshape them, edit them, or even delete them. It doesn't make them really go away, but it helps me feel like I have power over them, even if it's just metaphorical power.

Also, writing my fears helps me sort out where they come from. I find that if I start writing about my fears, even if I don't know what exactly they are, maybe just a hunch or an inkling of anxiety even, I can sort through the feelings and navigate the terrain a bit more. All I have to do is sit down and start typing. My fears or worries may make little sense when I begin, but on the page I'm able to get to the details that I didn't even know were there. Usually, that helps me make sense of their origins because sometimes that sneaks onto the page as well. Or, if I look back later at something I've written, I can see something I wasn't able to see at the time.

If you can dive in and begin grappling with the issues and ideas that have a hold on your mind, discovery is inevitable. Just as my student described above, sometimes details and insights emerge that you didn't know were there.

Another student wrote:

Confronting my fears in writing has opened up the possibility of being with fear in my life and therefore the opportunity to move through it. As I become more comfortable voicing how I'm feeling in my writing (especially what I see as the scary and ugly stuff), the further that stuff gets away from defining me as the awful subtext that never gets written. Fear becomes a part of my experience, not an unspeakable defining and overarching theme. I can write my fear honestly and then move through it.

It is scary to write our fears and worries and the "unspeakable." (*What will people think? How could I have felt that?*) Remember that you don't need to show anyone your writing—ever. But also know that if you do send into the world a piece of writing in which you have confronted your fears and the "unspeakable," you will, more often than not, receive e-mails and letters from readers thanking you for putting into words something about which most people don't write or speak.

Some of my students have been reluctant to write about their difficult moments as mothers—moments when maybe they didn't like being a mother, moments when they contemplated running out the front door to escape. But these are exactly the stories that need to be written so that other mothers know it's OK if they experience a similar thing. *You aren't crazy! You aren't a bad mother!* You're just having an off day or week or month. One of my students put it this way: "Every time someone has the courage and honesty to write about [situations and emotions] that are difficult, it normalizes the experience for another mother down the line. And our shame and fear and isolation get broken down a little more."

Another student, whose son has a rare genetic disorder, wrote the following:

> Very early on I was so afraid of my son and his devastating diagnosis that I wished he would die. As hard as it is to put those mother fears down, to see them typed on the page, I always feel like it is so important because I know there are other mothers out there who feel the same way and who will feel less alone if I share some of those difficult feelings. Writing about them allows me to own them, and then move on knowing that my authenticity will resonate with, and maybe help, someone else.

When the gritty, the heartbreaking, *and* the gorgeous and breathtaking parts of being a mother are given voice—and space—to exist side by side in literature, we can begin to chip away at the myths that surround motherhood. And coming face-to-face with our mother fears on the page can not only help us lay them to rest, it can help other mothers who might someday read our words.

WRITING EXERCISE:
MOTHER FEAR

For this exercise, make a list of fears and worries that have to do with your children. Pick one and describe your fear in as much detail as possible. Then describe what it feels like to be scared or consumed by worry like that. Be as concrete as you can, describing how your body feels. Pay attention to breathing and heart rate—the physical details. Then try to write about where this fear comes from. Can you place it? Do you know when you began to worry about it? If you feel you have hit on something worth exploring more in writing, try to write a scene having to do with this fear and really focus on sentence length. What happens to the feel of the scene if you run on and on? What happens when you make your sentences very short?

WRITING EXERCISE:
GETTING IT ALL DOWN

I very much admire writers who bravely get their emotions onto the page and who aren't afraid of exposing the sometimes ugly side of their human natures. I want you to try this. What are the things about yourself, your family, and your life that you are afraid to write or unwilling to write? Make a list. Then pick one and see what happens when you *do* write about it. Did your relationship with the material change in the act of writing? Are you still afraid of sharing it?

Our mother fears are sometimes based on our own experiences as children or adults. Perhaps you hope your children won't experience the same hardships and heartbreaks that you have endured. For instance, I hope my daughters will grow up confident in themselves and their skills and abilities. Part of this hope is rooted in the fact that I didn't feel this way until I was in my late twenties. I want them to believe in themselves always, to never question their worth. You can also think about this in terms of more systemic societal issues such as racism or gender equality or homophobia. How do we protect our children from these things? Is it possible? Erin White examines these questions in the following piece:

Book Bind

. . . .

"Can we read this?" Grace comes into the kitchen holding a book. She is still in her pajamas. I feel my heart tighten.

"Where did you find that?" I ask her.

"On your desk."

She is holding a book called *In Our Mothers' House* by Patricia Polacco. I bought the book last year because I loved the title and I love Patricia Polacco and the idea that she would write a book about a two-mom family seemed too good to be true. As it turned out it *was* too good to be true, which is why I had shuffled the book into the middle of a stack on my desk. The book is filled with beauty: a deeply joyful and loving family, a rambling old house in the Berkeley hills, charming details about food, pets, first steps, tree houses, family dinners. At its core the book is a love letter from a grown daughter to her mothers.

But it is also something else. Amidst the memories of pasta parties and banister-sliding there are also memories of a neighbor, a skinny woman with an angry face and wild blonde hair who wants to keep her children away from the narrator and her family. The first few times she appears her anger is subtle. She could be any old neighborhood grump. She frowns at the children's Halloween costumes and won't let her children sleep over in the community tree house with the rest of the neighborhood. But when the community comes together for a block party, the drama rises. The neighbor takes on the young girl's mothers. She yells at them, tells them to go away, and the illustrations show her hateful face and body, her children hiding behind her. Polacco depicts the mothers' pained faces, and the faces of their children crying.

Quickly the mothers offer their children comforting words about this woman not having any love in her heart and the story moves on to the children and their parents growing older. There are a few beautiful pages about weddings and grandchildren's first steps and burying the mothers on a hill near their home. The last page is a picture of children catching fireflies in the yard. And despite the fact that I am deeply frustrated with Polacco for succumbing to the age-old assumption that homophobia is the principal drama in the lives of children with lesbian mothers, the story still feels like a triumph.

And now here is Grace with the book in her hands. I don't want to read it to her, and yet I do want to, because it is far and away the most beautiful depiction of a two-mom family I have ever seen, and I know that she will love it. But I also know I can't read the page about the confrontation with the woman. So I read slowly and carefully. I read the pages in which the woman is just being grumpy. But when we get to the part about the block party, I hold the pages together and I turn ahead.

Grace loves the book. She wants me to read it again, and I do. She wants me to read it the next day, and the next, and early Saturday morning when I am rushing out the door to my yoga class. "When I get back," I tell her.

"I'll ask Mati," she says.

I panic. I haven't had time to talk about the book with Chris. "Grace wants you to read this book," I tell Chris. She is at the sink, filling the kettle. "But you can't read all the pages about the block party because—"

Grace walks in the room before I can finish and I have to resort to facial expressions and mouthing the word "homophobic neighbor" several times.

Chris looks at me. "It's 7 a.m. Could I just make some tea?"

For years we skipped over pages in books, although we hardly ever do it now. Now we read every page in *Martin's Big Words*, even the ones about him being shot. We read all of *When Marian Sang* (even though it is insanely long), including the pages about the receptionist at the music school who won't let Marian Anderson fill out an application because she is black. We even read Beatrix Potter's *The Tale of Samuel Whiskers* about the rats trying to make the Tom Kitten into pudding. But *In Our Mothers' House* is different. It tells the story of a family like ours, but with the addition of a hatred and anger that is completely foreign to Grace. Some might say that we don't know how lucky we are that this is true, and I would agree. But the luck is mine and Chris's, not Grace's. Grace's luck is that she has curly hair and a little sister and a star-shaped cookie in her lunch box every day. Her luck is a house on a dirt road with cows in the meadow and apples that hang low enough to pick. The fact that this house is in Massachusetts, a state where Chris and I can be married and have children that belong to both of us, that is our luck. And the hatred in the pages of Polacco's book, that is part of our story, not Grace's. Not yet.

I am not naïve: I know that someday—and it could be someday soon—Grace will be the target of an adult's anger and homophobia. Chris and I do everything we can to be certain that when that day comes she will know how to act and what to do. And our raising of her and June, the ways in which we prepare them for their lives in the greater and less accepting world, does not include the discussion of violence and hatred toward families like ours. Eventually the four of us will talk about such things, we will talk about Harvey Milk and Matthew Shepard. We will talk about Proposition 8 and Chris will tell the girls about the rainy afternoon in April when she rode the bus to the state house in Boston and saw young children hold signs saying "Gay Marriage is a Sin" while I stayed home because I was six months pregnant and frightened of what people might say to me.

But we won't tell them any of those things now. Right now we are working on helping Grace ride a two-wheeler and sound out words for a book she is writing about the bunny we are getting in the spring. Right now we are trying to convince June to sit on her Dora potty seat and stop hitting her friends when they take a toy away from her. Right now we are trying to convince both of them to eat something that is not a noodle covered in cheese.

Chris and I know the story Patricia Polacco is trying to tell. We know the story, and we know how it ends for some families and how it ends for others. And while we don't tell the story to our girls, we do carry it with us. The life we live is colored by the reality of prejudice, the possibility of harm. We manage these losses both publicly and privately, and Grace and June are witness to our choices and our actions, even now when they are too young to understand much of what we do and why we do it.

On Monday afternoon Grace is at school and June is napping. I am clearing off the dining room table and see the book. I open it, right to the page with the hateful neighbor. The illustration is so graphic, the children's faces so sad, there is no missing that something is terribly wrong. I don't know what to do: I love the story of this family, but soon enough Grace will be able to read the entire book herself. And before that, she might ask a babysitter to read it to her. The book starts to feel dangerous, which is an altogether terrible way for a book to feel. But it is dangerous: my daughter does not have any idea that there are people in this world who do not like her, who do not want to be near her, who do not think that she should have been born, because of who her parents are. I hold the book for a long time and then before I lose my nerve I open up Grace's art supply cabinet and take out a glue stick. I cover the woman's angry face with glue, I cover her cowering children, I cover the faces of the crying children. Then I push the pages together, and I smooth them between my hands, over and over, until they form one new page, only slightly thicker than the rest.

White writes that she and Chris will do everything they can to make sure their daughters will "know how to act and what to do" when they come face-to-face with homophobia. I think this piece raises an issue that we all wonder about as parents: How do we prepare our children for the world and its possible dangers while still allowing them to grow and explore and make their own way in life?

I also like this piece for how it encourages me to consider the ways that my children's stories might be different from mine. White writes, "the hatred in the pages of Polacco's book, that is part of our story, not Grace's." What is your children's luck and what is your luck? (In Chapter 9, Cecelie S. Berry addresses this question in terms of race.)

WRITING EXERCISE: MAMA SHIELD

What are the influences from which you want to shield your children? They might have to do with beliefs or experiences, or even something in your own past or family history that you want to keep from them until they are older. Pick one of these and write about it in as much detail as possible. How have your own experiences with it affected your hopes for your children? What kinds of choices have you made in order to protect your children?

CHAPTER 8

WRITING THE HARD STUFF

I can shake off everything if I write.
My sorrow disappears, my courage is reborn.
—ANNE FRANK

IN THE PROLOGUE TO HER MEMOIR-IN-PROGRESS, my former student Cindy Nerhbass writes how the memories of her daughter's near death are still palpable. Her daughter, born with Down syndrome and a hole in her heart, almost died in surgery when she was six months old. Fifteen years after the fact, Nerhbass writes, "no hours of therapy, no years passing, no counting of blessings, and no strength of will" can "render [these memories] benign." She goes on:

> My most useful tools, save God's grace, are pen and paper, the keyboard and screen. Wise teachers have guided, *Write about this; write about that.* And so, little by little, I must chip away at memory's fortress with chisels of words and empty spaces. This is the only true way out for a writer, isn't it? I will write and wait for

that transformational healing to begin, for the fog to dissipate and memories to relinquish their hold. Yet, all I can really say is this: *My daughter nearly died* (and this is the truth), *and it changed me forever.* Truth again.

At readings and in interviews over the years, I've heard writers—specifically writers of creative nonfiction—claim that the process of writing their stories wasn't therapeutic. I have seen them shake their heads, clearly offended at the suggestion. And I'm always curious about this; my guess is that they think if their writing is tied in any way to "therapy," it will somehow undercut the work they've put into crafting it.

But I believe that you can experience a transformation—a therapeutic transformation—in the writing process and still end up with art.

In his essay "The Fact Behind the Facts," Philip Gerard says that a memoir is "not simply a scrapbook of memories to brood over or cherish, but a *reckoning.* That's the reason to write a memoir: to find out what really happened in your life; to drive toward the fact behind all the other facts, and come to some understanding, however limited, of what it means—and accept that truth."

If you are truly doing this work of "reckoning," of diving in and fearlessly searching for the story in the material of your life, it's impossible for you *not* to make discoveries and gain perspective on the life you've lived. Isn't that process, at least on some level, therapeutic? Experiencing that does not detract from what an author has carefully crafted.

In every class I've taught I've had students grappling with the hard stuff—from postpartum depression and feelings of guilt and inadequacy to coming to terms with having a child with special needs to losing a child to illness or an accident. I have witnessed the crafting of beautiful writing from these losses, and I have heard how the process of writing helped these mothers come to terms with their heartbreak.

But writing can do more than help us, as writers, process and come to terms with the hard parts of motherhood and life; it can also change other mothers' lives. As my students mentioned in the previous chapter, when we read the struggles that other mothers have had, we know we're not alone in our own struggles, even if our challenges and heartbreaks are different. In the introduction to her anthology *Love You to Pieces: Creative Writers on Raising a Child with Special Needs*, Suzanne Kamata writes:

> I'm the kind of person who looks to literature to make sense of life, so when I learned that my daughter was deaf and had cerebral palsy, I sobbed for a while and then logged onto Amazon. com. I was looking for deep and sustaining stories to guide me on the long path ahead, and while I found many cheery volumes offering hope and inspiration, that wasn't exactly what I wanted. I needed to know that others had felt the same kind of pain, fear, and anger that I was feeling, and I wanted a better idea of how my daughter's disability would affect my marriage, my son, my work, and other aspects of our lives. The best novels, short stories, and memoirs can pull us into the lives of their characters and provide a deeper understanding of others, [and] poetry can distill and illuminate moments that longer essays gloss over.

She ends the introduction with this: "...literature eases loneliness and helps us understand and empathize with those unlike ourselves."

Reading a wide variety of voices and experiences—those of mothers and nonmothers alike—not only makes me a better mother; it makes me a better person. When I can walk in another person's shoes, my view of the world and its many joys and challenges expands. It makes me more compassionate and less judgmental, gives me an opportunity to connect with other people, regardless of where we came from and what we believe in. Always my hope in teaching and writing is that as mothers and people we can connect with and feel compassion for one another. I think we can, even when we don't agree.

One of the things to consider as you're writing the hard stuff is how to create enough emotional distance to be able to effectively tell your story. Just as Sonya Huber needed to find a way to talk about a subject that made her angry in a way that would invite readers in, you need to consider writing heartbreak with enough emotional distance so you don't overwhelm your readers.

Two ways to create emotional distance are with voice and tense. In Chapter 5 we discussed how voice can and often must be crafted to serve the purpose of a piece of writing. The following is a wonderful, but—brace yourself—heartbreaking piece by Susan Ito. Pay attention to the author's voice. How does she use Silverman's voices of innocence and experience to tell her story? Also notice tense. What tense does she use in each section? What effect does this have on the emotional content of the piece?

Samuel

. . . .

I remember almost nothing about that pregnancy except the way that it ended. I remember a walk along the grassy trails of Sea Ranch, the wild wind, my bursting energy. I was wearing my husband, John's, blue jeans to accommodate my five-month pregnant belly.

In August, we took a trip to the beach with his brother's family. I swelled in the humidity like a sponge, my breasts enormous, my face squishy with fluid. "Look at me," I said, frowning in the mirror. "You look wonderful," he said. It wasn't what I was talking about.

John, a doctor, went from that family vacation to El Salvador, heading a medical delegation to the war zone of Guazapa, under the volcano. My father-in-law disapproved, told me outright that he felt John was abandoning me. But I was proud. While he was in Central America, I drove to Davis to help load a container of wheelchairs, crutches, and medicine bound for Nicaragua. It was then that I noticed I couldn't lace my sneakers. My feet were the size of small footballs.

I picked him up at the airport, saying, "Don't you think I look fat?"

"You're pregnant, sweetheart," he said. "That's how you're supposed to look."

Sunday, September 17, 1989. I had gained thirteen pounds in a week. I pulled out the pregnancy book. In red print, it said, *Call the doctor if you gain more than three pounds in one week. If your face or hands or feet are swollen.* If. If. If. I checked them all off. While John was in the shower, I called my obstetrician and friend, Lisa. I whispered under the sound of running water, "I think something is wrong."

Lisa's voice was so smooth, so calm. "Swelling is very common," she said, "but it would be a good idea to get a blood pressure check. Can John do it?"

We stopped by his office, two blocks from the restaurant we had decided on for dinner. We were planning a movie, a bookstore; our usual date. I hopped onto the exam table, held out my arm. I couldn't wait to get to la Méditerranée. My mouth had been dreaming of spanakopita all day.

I heard the Velcro tearing open on the cuff, felt its smooth blue band wrapping around me. I swung my feet and smiled up at John, the stethoscope around his neck, loved this small gesture of taking care of me. I felt the cuff tightening, the pounding of my heart echoing up and down my fingers, through my elbow.

The expression on his face I will never forget, the change in color from pink to ash, as if he had died standing at my side. "Lie down," he said quietly. "Lie down on your left side. *Now.*"

The numbers were all wrong, two hundred plus, over and over again, his eyes darkening as he watched the mercury climb on the wall. He shook his head. "What's Lisa's phone number?"

His voice was grim as he spoke to her on the phone—numbers, questions, a terrible urgency. He told me to go into the tiny bathroom and pee into a cup. "We've got to dipstick your urine, see if there's any protein."

I sat on the toilet and listened to him crash through the cupboards, knocking over samples of ulcer pills, brochures about stomach cancer, looking for a container of thin paper tabs. I gave him the paper cup, the gold liquid cloudy and dense. The dipstick changed color quickly, from white to powdery blue to sky to deep indigo. My protein level was off the chart. "No," he whispered. "No, no, goddammit, no."

I asked what, over and over, not believing, as he pulled me out the door, across the street to the hospital. He pounded the buttons of the elevator, pulled me flying to the nurses' station, spat numbers at them. I thought, *Don't be a bully, nurses hate doctors who are bullies;* but they scattered like quail, one of them on the phone, another pushing me, stumbling, into a room. There were three of them, pulling at my clothes, my shoes; the blood pressure cuff again; the shades were drawn; they moved so swiftly, with such seriousness.

I had a new doctor now. Lisa, obstetrician of the normal, was off my case, and I was assigned a special neonatologist named Weiss. He was perfectly bald, with thick glasses, and wooden clogs, a soft voice.

A squirt of blue gel on my belly for the fetal monitor, the galloping sound of hoofbeats, the baby riding a wild pony inside me. What a relief to hear that sound, although I didn't need the monitor; I could feel the baby punching at my liver.

There was a name for what I had. Preeclampsia. Ahh. Well, preeclampsia was certainly better than eclampsia, and as long as it was pre, then they could stop it, couldn't they? And what was eclampsia? An explosion of blood pressure, a flood of protein poisoning the blood, kidney failure, the vessels in spasm, a stroke, seizures, blindness, death. But I didn't have any of those things. I had *pre*eclampsia. It felt safe.

They slipped a needle into my wrist, hung a bag of magnesium sulfate. This is to prevent seizures, they said. You may feel a little hot. As the first drops of the drug slipped into my bloodstream, I felt a flash of electricity inside my mouth. My tongue was baking. My scalp prickled, burning, and I threw up onto the sheets. I felt as if I was being microwaved.

I was wheeled down to radiology. Pictures of the baby onscreen, waving, treading water. A real child, not a pony or a fish. The x-ray tech, a woman with curly brown hair and a red Coca-Cola t-shirt, asked, "Do you want to know the sex?" I sat up. "There you go." She pointed. A flash between the legs, like a finger. A boy. I nearly leapt off the gurney. "John! Did you see? A boy! It's Samuel!" Sahm-*well*, the Spanish pronunciation, named after our surrogate father in Nicaragua, the most dignified man we knew.

He didn't want to look, couldn't celebrate having a son. He knew so much more than I did.

Weiss came to stand next to my bed. Recited numbers slowly.

"Baby needs at least two more weeks for viability. He's already too small, way too small. But you..." He looked at me sadly, shook his head. "You probably can't survive two weeks without having a stroke, seizures, worse." He meant I could die.

"What are the chances...that we could both make it?" Doctors are always talking percentages.

"Less than ten percent, maybe less than five percent." The space between his fingers shrunk into nothing.

This is how they said it. I was toxemic, poisoned by pregnancy. My only cure was to not be pregnant anymore. The baby needed two more weeks, just fourteen days.

I looked at John hopefully. "I can wait. It will be all right."

"Honey. Your blood pressure is through the roof. Your kidneys are shutting down. You are *on the verge of having a stroke.*"

I actually smiled at him. I actually said that having a stroke at twenty-nine would not be a big deal. I was a physical therapist; I knew about rehab. I could rehabilitate myself. I could walk with a cane. Lots of people do it. I had a bizarre image of leaning on the baby's carriage, supporting myself the way elderly people use a walker.

We struggled through the night. "I'm not going to lose this baby," I said.

"I'm not going to lose *you*," he said.

He won.

I lay with my hands on my belly all night, feeling Samuelito's limbs turning this way and that. There was nothing inside me that could even think of saying goodbye.

September 18, 1989. Another day of magnesium sulfate, the cuff that inflated every five minutes, the fetal monitor booming through the room. No change in status for either of us.

I signed papers of consent, my hand moving numbly across the paper, my mind screaming, I do *not* consent, I do *not*, I do not.

In the evening, Weiss's associate entered with a tray, a syringe, and a nurse with mournful eyes.

"It's just going to be a bee sting," he said.

And it was, a small tingle, quick pricking bubbles, under my navel; and then a thing like a tiny drinking straw that went in and out with a barely audible pop. It was so fast. I thought, *I love you, I love you, you must be hearing this, please hear me.* And then a Band-Aid was unwrapped, with its plastic smell of childhood, and spread onto my belly.

"All done," he said. All done.

My child was inside swallowing the fizzy drink, and it bubbled against his tiny tongue like a bud, the deadly soda pop.

This is what it was. A drug, injected into my womb, a drug to stop his heart. To lay him down to sleep, so he wouldn't feel what would happen the next day, the terrible terrible thing that would happen. *Evacuation* is what it is called in medical journals.

Evacuees are what the Japanese Americans were called when they were ripped from their homes, tagged like animals, flung into the desert. Evacuated, exiled, thrown away.

I lay on my side pinching the pillowcase. I wondered if he would be startled by the drug's taste, if it was bitter, or strange, or just different from the salt water he was used to. I prayed that it wouldn't be noxious, not like the magnesium sulfate, that it wouldn't hurt. That it would be fast.

John sat next to the bed and held one hand as I pressed the other against my belly. I looked over his shoulder into the dark slice of night between the heavy curtains. Samuel, Samuelito, jumped against my hand once. He leaped through the space into the darkness and then was gone.

All gone.

* * *

I have two other children now, daughters. I love them with every cell in my body. And yet I do not forget that son, small cowboy, the way he galloped through me. There is still a part of me that believes that I failed the test of motherhood, the law that says your child comes before you, even if it means death. I look at my girls, the life that fills this family, and I think, none of this would be here. But still.

I wonder about our life with a boy, what it would have been. Now John often steps into the tension-filled space between my teenage daughters and me, as we work out our complicated mother–daughter dance. I wonder if he and Sam, Samuel, Samuelito, would have had this flinty hardness between them. I wonder if they would have played sports together, if they would have gone camping and fishing.

I have looked at a thousand boys, from toddlers to young men, since that day in 1989, and none of them have come close to the perfection of that unlived life, that beautiful son who never took a breath. I know how completely unfair it is, and yet I do it, have done it over and over. Our Sam, our Sammy, would never have pointed a stick like a weapon, would never have pulled the legs from an insect. He would have been an avid reader. He would have loved to learn, but not in a nerdy way. He would have been easy with his friends, sweet with his mother, bonded with his father. He would have grown up to be a camp counselor, a scientist, a pediatrician.

How much simpler it is to love a ghost, an angel of a child, than one who is troublesomely human and alive.

The night his heart ceased to beat, I had an image of him that I flash to even now. I could see the person he would one day grow into, tousled, with dark, damp almost-curls stuck to his forehead. But he wouldn't smell bad, no; he would smell alive, human. A slightly torn, stretched-out t-shirt, something faded with a clever, ironic saying on it. He would have just stopped shooting hoops in the brick courtyard and would be resting at the bottom of the rickety, age-worn stairs. He would be drinking Coke from an old-fashioned green glass bottle like someone from a well-directed commercial. He would stop to look at me, in an instant of unembarrassed sweetness.

None of this is true.

If Samuel had lived, he would have smelled bad. He would have sworn and slammed the door and left his foul socks underneath the couch. He would have had times of sullenness. He would have fought with members of his family. He would have been far from perfect, as we all are. He would have been a complex, living person with qualities that are, at this moment, absolutely unknowable.

There are a million questions that will forever go unanswered. I wonder how I would fare as a mother of a boy. I am innately unathletic, and squeamish about the amphibians and insects that so many boys seem to love. But is that just a stereotype? Thinking that he would have grown up to be an athletic, frog-loving type of boy?

I often wonder how things would be different if he had survived that blast of preeclampsia and been born that September in 1989. He would have been miniscule, no larger than a baked potato. There would have been months in a neonatal intensive-care unit;

possible (no, probable) complications. He might very well have had disabilities, from mild to unthinkably severe. And what kind of mother would this have made me? Heartbroken? Overwhelmed? Hoveringly protective?

When my daughters were born healthy, I was intensely grateful just that they were alive. It gave me the sense that they had made it through their uterine gauntlet and could thus dodge anything. Instead of becoming the hovering, worrying mother I might have been with a little preemie like Samuel, I became oddly relaxed. I didn't fret and cling like some other parents I knew. I let them go off to sleepaway circus camp when they were seven years old and most of their classmates hadn't even mastered one-night sleepovers. Perhaps, knowing that one of my children had already been taken from me, I believed that the powers that be wouldn't dream of taking another.

I've heard so often that parenting boys is utterly different from parenting girls, and I can only imagine the ways this might be true in our family. I know that sometimes the concentration of estrogen in the air can be stifling, and that the drama meter around here feels like it is permanently set to high. Would this have been different with a boy, and particularly with a boy named Samuel?

I wonder what kind of brother he would have been. I know that his sisters could not possibly be more different—physically or temperamentally. Would he have been dark and intense like our elder girl, or fair and mellow like the younger?

The questions swirl around and around; they break apart like atoms and produce even more questions. The answers are infinite and untouchable.

In the end, all I can really know about this child is that he would have been a boy. And he would have been loved.

This essay brings tears to my eyes each time I read it. As a preeclampsia survivor I know what could have happened if I hadn't been as far along as I was in my pregnancy with Stella, so I have a visceral reaction to so much of what Ito writes in this piece.

VOICE

Ito's voice changes from the beginning of the piece to the end, which helps readers understand the impact of the loss of Samuel in her life. In the first section, she very much resides in the voice of innocence, and in the second section, she moves into a reflective voice of experience. One of my students wrote this in response to "Samuel":

> In the first section, [Ito's] voice shifts from carefree, almost whimsical, to desperate, disbelieving, and even despondent, which matches the content of the story she is telling: she is a "carefree" pregnant woman, and then she is a desperate one in despair who passes through a period of disbelief, shock. Her voice matches the condition of her pregnancy and changes with it... In the second part of the essay, her voice...reveals a woman who has had time to digest her loss... Here, her voice is one of acceptance, of a woman who has grown and lived and loved and come to terms with a tragic loss.

Another student described how Ito's word choice at the beginning of the piece lets the reader know that Ito isn't yet worried, though she should be. We are residing in Ito's voice of innocence when she uses language like "hopped onto the exam table," and "I swung my feet." My student pointed out that Ito's sentences "get longer and more fragmented when they reach the hospital. And [Ito holds] on to her innocence during that whole paragraph about preeclampsia: 'But I didn't have any of those things. I had *pre*eclampsia. It felt safe.' Then [we see] her voice of experience at the end of this section: 'He didn't want to look, couldn't celebrate having a son. He knew so much more than I did.'"

TENSE

Tense is another element to think about when you're writing the hard stuff. One of the things that makes "Samuel" accessible to readers is Ito's use of past tense in the section where she loses Samuel. Then in the subsequent section, she moves into present tense, describing her life without Samuel. In the latter section, her "now" self reflects on the preeclampsia and loss of Samuel. She is still thinking these thoughts, still living with this loss, years after the fact. This is a reflective present tense because what she is reflecting on is something that happened in the past. Much of the reflection in memoir happens when the "now" self, the self who is writing and thinking about thoughts and events, enters the piece and thinks these things aloud on the page. We noticed Jill Christman doing this in "The Allergy Diaries" in sentences like "Sometimes Mark and I wonder what our lives would be like if I had actually gotten on the plane on that morning in February..." Christman uses past tense conditional because she's talking about a hypothetical situation in the past. Then she moves into straight past tense to tell the story until the shift into present tense at the moment of crisis.

A benefit of using past tense is that it can give you a little emotional distance. Writing in the present tense can sometimes be more painful because you have to inhabit the scene in a different way. I've had students try difficult scenes in present tense and then abandon the present because it felt too close. They didn't want to go back to that time and relive it the way they felt they needed to do in present tense.

Best-selling author Hope Edelman said something similar when I interviewed her about her memoir *The Possibility of Everything*:

The story in the book took place in 2000, but I chose to write it in the present tense, which meant going back and inhabiting the voice and persona of who I was back then: a very anxious new mom and not a particularly grateful wife. Although my friends back then might not agree, I think I was in some ways not a very nice person nine years ago, and it pained me to come face-to-face with that while telling my story. I made the choice to depict myself honestly rather than trying to sugarcoat some of my less-flattering moments because I wanted to be fair and accurate to readers, but boy, it was really hard to avoid passing judgment on myself. Ultimately I had to come to a place of compassion for the lost, struggling, imperfect woman, mother, and wife I was back then.

Edelman wrote her memoir in a crafted present tense. By that I mean that we know the events she is writing about are in the past—they've already happened—but she has chosen to tell them in the present tense for the immediacy that it gives a piece of writing. This is called immersion present tense.

Immersion present tense can heighten the narrative urgency, but it changes how the voices of experience and innocence enter into the piece and can make it more difficult to reflect on the page. For instance, my memoir is in immersion present tense, so when I reflect and sometimes foreshadow, I must use future tense:

> Months later I'll wonder at my lack of tears... I'll realize that even with the books spread before me spelling out our future, even as I contemplated eclampsia as a possibility, I didn't think my pregnancy would end that way—in seizures, in growth retardation, in premature birth.

This is a glimpse into the perspective of the "now" me writing the book, looking back, wondering at my (lack of) reaction.

Even though immersion present tense makes the events you are reading about feel more immediate, you have to give readers (and yourself) breathing room so it's not overwhelming. One way to do this is to inject moments of humor, as I describe doing in my memoir, or to dip into backstory or research to help relieve some of the narrative pressure. I try to balance the intense chapters with chapters that allow you to learn more about Donny and me and our lives before children.

One thing to keep in mind if you choose to write in present tense is that sometimes it's difficult for the reader to gauge how far removed you are from the experiences about which you're writing. A couple of years ago I wrote an essay about experiencing postpartum intrusive thoughts in the weeks after Zoë was born. (It was actually quite scary; I worried that I would throw her to the ground. Logically, I knew I wouldn't do this, but the thought of doing it—the possibility that I might be physically capable of it—was terrifying. I experienced this after Stella was born as well, but it was more intense with Zoë.) I wrote an essay about this in present tense, but when my writing group read it they were ready to have me committed—they couldn't tell from the writing whether I was OK or not. I subsequently changed the whole piece to past tense to give the reader (and myself) a little breathing room and to let the reader know that Zoë and I had made it through those weeks.

So play with tense and see what happens. If you are writing about a very difficult situation, maybe try it in past tense first. Ease yourself into the scene. Then, if you think it would benefit from the immediacy of present tense, change it.

WRITING EXERCISE: FROM PAST TO PRESENT

Pick something that you wrote in past tense that feels flat or distant or doesn't ring true. Read it over once or twice, and then put it to the side. Now rewrite it in present tense. Try to inhabit the scene and who you were at the time it occurred. Use as many details as possible. When you're finished, compare the two versions. How are they different? How are they the same?

WRITING EXERCISE:
JUST THE FACTS

Sometimes when you are writing about an emotionally charged situation, it helps to first get the facts down on paper. Take a few minutes to think about something (a situation or scene) that you're having trouble writing, that is difficult because you don't know how to approach it or because there is too much emotion there. It doesn't have to be extreme. It doesn't even have to be about your child.

Once you have the scene or situation in mind, list the facts. For instance, if I were going to do this with the first time I saw Stella after her birth, I would begin like this:

I wore two hospital gowns, one opening at my back and one opening at my front.

Donny pushed the wheelchair.

The tunnel to Children's Hospital was hot and bright.

I clutched the arms of the wheelchair, dizzy. I thought I might fall out, spill onto the floor.

The NICU smelled sweet.

Stella was 42 hours old.

She lay on an open warming table at Station 5.

Once you have a long list of facts—no emotions—write the scene. Begin with "I remember…" Repeat this whenever you get stuck. Try not to incorporate any emotional words (*upset, angry, love, devastated*). Try to convey feeling through the way you write the facts.

CHAPTER 9

WHERE IS YOUR MIND?: REFLECTION IN CREATIVE NONFICTION

MY YOUNGER DAUGHTER, ZOË, LOVES TO SWING AT the park. With each push, her tangled red hair flies into her face and then out behind her like a flag. "Higher, Mama. Higher!" she squeals. And when I'm not entertaining her with silly, tripping "side dogs" (my pathetic, goofy version of an underdog), I let the rocking rhythm of my body, forward and back, forward and back, remind me of the times when my mom brought my sisters and me to this very same park as little girls. I remember the way Rachel and I trailed after our older sister, Sara, trying to keep up as she scrambled through the cement tubes and up the rocket climber (both of which have long since been replaced). I remember the sand in our hair, and how our knees became red and raw from falls in the cement tubes.

These memories might lead me to thinking of the house on Wheeler Street and how—in those innocent-seeming years before my parents' divorce—I loved to lie on the floor as a five-year-old and watch the particles of dust float through the afternoon sun. But then I wonder: were those years really innocent? Or could my sisters and I sense that our parents' marriage wasn't a happy one?

I'm pulled back to present day at the park when Zoë again squeals, "Higher, Mama!" I lean into the push and say, "Hold on tight, sweetie." And off she goes, flying high in front of me, laughing her wild, infectious laugh.

In "Memory and Imagination," Patricia Hampl writes, "Memoir is the intersection of narration and reflection [...] It can present its story and consider the meaning of the story." In Chapter 2, I mentioned that reflection is one of the four key characteristics of memoir and personal essay. Reflection adds depth and meaning to a piece of writing.

In creative nonfiction you can be doing one thing—the staged action of a piece—while the real action is happening in your head. In those short paragraphs about pushing Zoë at the park, the park is the stage: I am pushing my daughter on the swing. But the real action— where the story is going to unfold and where I will begin to process that story—is in my head.

The following poem by Nicole Collins Starsinic about her relationship with her stepdaughter is a great example of staged action versus internal action:

How the story begins

Two years after she moved out (abruptly)
I wipe the cutting board clean,
crumbs falling into a clump in my hand,
and I am startled into remembering her at nine
energy humming from her restless limbs,
dusty boots swinging from the counter,
as she followed me from room to room
settling in the kitchen to watch me chop and slice.

And sometimes
if the light from the window fell
just so upon the counter
and if the week at her mom's
hadn't turned her completely
against me
she'd beg me to tell her
just one more story...

And because I'd learned to hoard the crumbs
others had the luxury to discard
I'd take the moment as proof
(trying not to be too greedy)
that all this was not in vain.

How every story began
Once there was a girl named...

Just as I was drawn back to my childhood as I pushed Zoë at the park, Starsinic is pulled back to early stepmotherhood as she brushes crumbs from the cutting board. The narrator is in the kitchen, doing what she's done a hundred times. But the story is in her memory; it's about her relationship with her stepdaughter and not taking any moment with her stepdaughter for granted. As was discussed in Chapter 2, the real story in creative nonfiction is often internal; it's about a shift in perspective or a new way of seeing or making sense of the world. And in order to tap into this part of the story, you need to be able to reflect.

WRITING EXERCISE:
WHERE IS MY MIND?

Make a list of tasks that you do often—cook, play with your kids, grocery-shop, fold laundry, shuttle children to practices and appointments, and so on. Pick a moment when you were in the middle of one of these tasks but your thoughts were far away, and write the scene in as much detail as possible. Then zoom in on what you were thinking about. What's the story going on in your head? How does the current scene intrude on your thoughts? Write for 15 or 20 minutes, letting the story in your head be grounded in the action of the scene.

PLACE AND REFLECTION

Great places for reflection in writing are standing at windows, driving in cars, walking. (These are also great places for a sentence or two of summary or backstory.) Place (setting) is often an effective trigger for reflection, and in my own writing I've found that recollecting a scene where I'm in a place that is important to me is often an effective avenue into reflection.

Here is a scene from my memoir as an example of "placed" reflection. This scene takes place about a week and a half after Stella was born. My mom has driven me out to the suburbs, to the house where Donny and I lived for three and a half years after we were married. In exchange for rent, Donny and I helped the owner, Mimi, around her house and took her on errands. My favorite task was watering the orchids in Mimi's greenhouse. (At this point in the memoir I am struggling with not yet feeling like a mother. There is a new couple—Kim and Dave—who are living with Mimi, and I've just had a very short haircut.)

Mom and I let ourselves in through the garage, just as Donny and I did when we lived here. As we walk into the familiarity of Mimi's kitchen, I'm struck by how much my life has changed in the last few months. Yet as I move through her kitchen and into her living room, I feel myself sliding back in time, into my role as Mimi's caretaker.

"Kate!" she cries when she sees me.

I lean down and give her a hug, kissing her papery cheek.

"Your hair!" she says. Then, "I've been worried sick!" As if these two things are connected.

"I cut it." Then, "I know. I'm sorry."

"What can I get you? Tea? Coffee?" She looks from my mom to me, placing her hands on the arms of her chair as if she's planning to stand.

"No, no," I say, waving my hand. "I'll get it. How about tea?" I slip on a cheerfulness that I haven't felt in weeks and move into her kitchen, where I put water on the stove and pull mugs and boxes of tea from the cupboards. I line everything up on a tray. And it's odd, but I really do feel almost cheerful. I can see why people "stay busy" when their lives are falling apart. It's so much easier than thinking about what's happening and about how little control you have over it.

I stand in front of the stove as the pot of water begins to sizzle and crack. From the other room I hear my mom talking about Stella, about the book she reads to her in the mornings on her way to work. I could go back into the living room and describe the texture of my new life, but instead I lean against the counter and stare out the window at Mimi's wooded lot, where three cardinals perch at the bird feeder. I can't count the number of times I hauled birdseed to that feeder. It made Mimi crazy when the squirrels and raccoons would eat the seed, and she was always devising new methods to repel them. One time, she insisted I rub olive oil and cayenne pepper on the feeder post. But it didn't work. Nothing worked.

Oddly, I miss hauling birdseed. I miss taking Mimi's dog, Maggie, for a walk every day. I miss all the clear-cut jobs I had while Donny and I lived here. I knew what to do. I knew what Mimi needed. I made a difference.

When the water boils, I pour it over the tea bags, and carry the tray with the cups and a plate of cookies into the living room. My mom shows Mimi the photos she's taken of Stella, the ones in which Stella is still very yellow, Velcro goggles dangling from her temple. "Oh, Kate," Mimi says over and over.

"I know," I say, between bites of my cookie. "But she's doing okay. The doctor said she might move back to the Special Care nursery in a week."

Mimi nods. "I have something for her." She points to a huge gift bag on the floor next to her chair, and slides it toward me. I sit with it at my feet and pull out onesies and blankets and frilly bibs and burp cloths covered in butterflies—all pink and purple and flowered.

"This is excessive," I say. And I know that she made Kim drive her to Babies R Us. I can imagine Mimi leaning on the shopping cart, pointing to item after item. I know she did this even though she hasn't been feeling well. "Thank you," I say as I hug Mimi. "They're perfect."

Mimi shrugs. "Go take a look at the greenhouse," she says. "Kim and Dave are doing a wonderful job. But I think the orchids miss you."

I push open the glass door and step down into the greenhouse and take a deep breath. The warm, humid air and the scent of dirt fill my lungs. How many hours did I spend here during the three and a half years that Donny and I lived with Mimi? Certainly over a hundred. Now, a couple dozen orchids are in bloom and their yellow and violet and scarlet petals are like shouts amid a quiet sea of green. I walk slowly around the center table, lifting leaves to check for parasitic scale. I flick one onto the floor with my thumbnail. Then I walk along the outside wall, where the Vandas, my favorite orchids—and Mimi's as well—perch along the window like gangly prehistoric birds. One of them is about to bloom, and through the pale green of the buds I can tell the petals will be magenta.

Mimi always gave me credit when her orchids bloomed. "Kate, you're a genius," she'd say. I would smile and shrug off her compliment, but secretly I was pleased that she thought I was responsible for the silky petals, for the blasts of color. Week after week I groomed and watered these plants, but I didn't do anything special. Mostly, I just watched and waited.

And suddenly, as I stand in Mimi's greenhouse, surrounded by all that throbbing color, I understand that this is what I must do with Stella, as well. I must wait. I must be patient. And eventually, she will come home. Eventually I will feel like her mother.

Much of the real action here takes place in my head. But it helps to "place" my thoughts in a physical space. I am making connections between my life before Stella and my current life as the mother to a sick, hospitalized infant. The reader also has a chance to learn something of my life before Stella in my interactions with Mimi.

Why and when you remember certain things is sometimes as important as the memory itself. Our take on these memories is always changing because we are always changing. Memoir is about the relation between the self and a specific subject, and this relationship is part of the story. But though the subject may remain the same, the self (and all its perspectives and thoughts) is always changing. So some important questions to consider when you're reflecting in your writing are: Why is this memory or recollection or thought important to me now? What is happening in my life now to take me back to a certain memory or moment? What is happening with my "now" writing self that raises the stakes where this memory is concerned? Asking these questions will help you dive under the surface of your writing.

When you are reflecting in your writing and moving back in time with memories, it's important always to ground the reader in time. Remember how Chitra Divakaruni grounded us at her mother's house in Gurap before dipping into backstory and taking us on a journey of scents and memories? She moves around in time in that piece but we are not lost, because she grounds us in a specific time and place: the visit to her mother's house in Gurap with her sons.

In order to make reflection and the incorporation of backstory easier and to not confuse your reader, it helps to settle on the stage of your piece. From there, you can move back and forward in time to expand the reach of the narration. I have a former student who wrote a piece about riding a roller coaster (even though roller coasters terrified her) three days after her daughter died of SIDS. The stage of the piece is the mall, three days after her daughter's death. But the piece feels bigger when the author fleshes out the stage with reflection and backstory (details about her life, her daughter's life, her daughter's death). She can also move into future tense to provide a sense of what the coming days and months will bring, and explain (though she didn't understand it at the time) why she went on that roller coaster: to shock herself out of a state of numbness, to feel something, even if it was terror. She can do all of this because she solidly grounds us in the *when* of the stage.

WHAT SHAPES US:
REFLECTION AND MOTHERHOOD

In Chapter 3 I discussed how our own mothers and cultural ideals of motherhood affect who we are as mothers. I want to broaden this question to ask what other factors in our lives, such as religion, class, or race, helped shape who we are as mothers.

The following piece by Cecelie S. Berry addresses how race and the fact that Berry is African American affected her growing up, and how it works in her mothering:

Was He Black or White?

A few years ago, my sons and I were having a dinner when Sam, who was then eight years old, told us about Dominick, a second-grade classmate known for his disruptive antics. When the Spanish teacher's back was turned, Dominick would rise and canter about the classroom, twirling an invisible lasso above his head. A God-fearing child, he punctuated the close of the circle with a rip-roaring "Hallelujah!" My six-year-old, Spenser, and I fell out laughing as Sam mimicked Dominick's escapades. When the laughter died down, a termite-sized query gnawed at me, so I asked, "Is Dominick black or white?"

Silence. Sam and Spenser looked at each other, a tacit conference. They were closing ranks and taking arms.

"What difference does it make?" Sam asked.

"It doesn't make any difference. I just want to know," I replied.

"But everybody's the same. So it doesn't matter." Spenser now.

"I'm just curious."

"Why're you curious?"

"Because I want to know." Great storm clouds thundered across their shared gaze: *Mommy is a racist.*

"I just want to be able to picture what was happening, that's all. Now, was he white or black?"

They crossed their arms. I crossed my legs. The stir-fry curdled. Everybody pushed back from the table.

I drew the ace card: "I'm your mother. Tell me now."

Even as the conversation unfolded, I knew that it would change us. It was a turning point in the compass of our relationship: a black mother and her children having careless fun, and then the issue of race spins us clockwise and counter—I'm still not sure which. That night, I stumbled upon the mores of a new generation that believed—they didn't just say it, *they believed*—that race didn't matter. My children's utter faith in this impressed me. They exhibited unwavering conviction and—warming to a mother's heart, if contrary to my will—they were fierce allies, utterly united. They fought me (me!) for an ideal world where they were ultimately human, and race was simply not worth mentioning.

I had discovered the vast new territory of their idealism, as unspoiled and fertile as the Americas must have been to explorers of yore. Appraising that Xanadu, I stuck my flag of racial awareness deep and declared it mine. Is my influence civilizing or am I—a black woman, the earth's earth mother—just another conquering barbarian? I wonder still.

Sam, ever loyal to his mother, gave in. "He was black."

"You see?" I said brightly. "It's really no big deal." I shrugged elaborately, but I could see they didn't believe me. One of the veils from behind which we mothers appear so perfect had slipped away that evening. They saw me a mite more clearly as a flawed and perhaps even dangerous person.

Look, we all do it, don't we? We take note of who does what and what color they are, comparing them to what we know and expect, sizing them up to our understanding of their kind, the world. My sons felt that the mere mention of race poised one, teetering, on the slippery slope to bigotry. I did not agree. It's human nature to form some lexicon for understanding other people, and race—a sociological construct, not a scientific term—has traditionally been one. We use it to help us get a handle on the situation, to think we know whom we're dealing with.

It is how we behave when our attitudes and expectations go unmet—when the person standing before us had defied the rules that supposedly define his or her group—that tests us. It is the line of demarcation between how much we are trying to understand the world and how much we are trying to make it conform to our understanding.

When a white workman I called to fix a broken pane of glass arrives and rings our bell, he stares angrily at me for answering the door. He did not expect me. He has taken note of what is on the news, what he has heard and observed. He thought black people were in the ghetto and laid claim to an assumption that he is not entitled to but made him more at home in the world.

Nobody takes note of race more than we African Americans. A particularly gruesome crime occurs—the killing rampage of the "D.C. sniper," for instance. The tacit but almost universal assumption among blacks was that the sniper must be white "'cause we don't roll like that." The idea that blacks were less prone to this kind of crime made us feel safer, even morally one-up to whites. When the sniper turned out to be black, we found ourselves more vulnerable to the idea that we, too, can produce and be victimized by serial killers.

African Americans feel the loss of these assumptions acutely. Our habits and cultural predilections have traditionally been our fortress, where we could feel at ease in a hostile land. To preserve that sense of security, we can be merciless enforcers of the rule: Our speech, dress, interests are expected to conform to the topography of "blackness" as we know it. In my mid-twenties, I attended the family reunion of a black friend and when asked how I wanted my steak prepared, I requested it medium rare. "Oooooh," a woman ejaculated, a sirenlike noise assuring that all eyes would turn in our direction. "Only white folks like their meat rare. We black folks like our meat well done."

My life had been incalculably altered by the fact of race. I am not angry about it; being born black in 1961 to educated, ambitious, and committed parents, I led a life that was in many ways charmed. I was poised to take advantage of the movements—civil rights, women's liberation, affirmative action—that provided opportunities my ancestors had dared not dream of. From the beginning, I sensed that it would be my generation's challenge to fully tame the wilderness of race, to build a "settlement" for blacks in America where we could *completely* embrace ourselves. That step taken, we could stand as equals and embrace others regardless of their skin color. It is a journey that generations before initiated and one that I continue now as a mother. Having taken up those reins, I have turned often for direction from the map my parents drew up for me, veering from it as needed.

My parents, who bore the burdens of growing up in segregation, raised us according to the exacting gaze of the white eyeball. They knew that to get ahead, we would have to be fluent in classical music, ballet, everything in the European tradition—to show white America we knew what counted. Fervent integrationists, my parents resembled most ambitious black people of the Greatest Generation. They resented, feared, and always distrusted whites, but noted that the rare black person crowned as worthy was the anti-black, so they poured us into that mold. There were costs to many families. Nightmarish, secret costs: "too dark" siblings being marginalized; the very light ones passing into oblivion as they passed for white. And always, no matter what your shade, there was the pressure to conceal your interest in "black" things: tap dancing, basketball, gospel music.

The pressure to assimilate mounted after we moved from a street of respectable, middle-class Negroes in Cleveland to the predominantly white, affluent suburb of Shaker Heights in 1971. We lived in the center of town, so far from the vast majority of black families that we often felt like exiles in a strange, lovely Siberia. I suppose that is why, on Sundays, my dad would often listen to black gospel music on the radio. It was, in part, the black church and the influence of black music that enabled him to rise from being a poor foster child to a successful internist. While he and Mother knew we had to move up—and urged us to adopt the "white" interests and mannerisms and friends to do so—my dad quietly resented that certain "black" things would necessarily be jettisoned along the way: gospel music and a whole array of high-cholesterol foods among them. That music—like the smell of chitlins cooking—sent us kids diving under pillows. The sound molested us, leaving echoes of guilt and confusion. It made us *uncomfortable*. The more uncomfortable we were, the louder Dad played it.

One day—I might have been fourteen then—a screaming fight broke out between my father and mother because Dad was playing gospel music so loud that it seemed our white neighbors (a Cleveland Clinic doctor, a law firm partner) could hear. Mother marched downstairs, snapped off the radio, and cursed Dad out in tones so voluble, I couldn't help but wonder why it didn't concern her that the neighbors might hear *that*. Eventually, Dad stopped listening to gospel music. He had a life we children knew very little about—one that included a "blackness" my mother despised and was determined, not altogether without cause, to banish from our lives.

Truthfully, I don't think my parents ever felt completely comfortable with or even fully recognized the complex duality of our lives, or the toll that never fitting into either world would take on us children. They had tried to give us a better life and were confused by our flailing, identity struggles, and discontent. Who and what was responsible for our unhappiness remains a source of division in our family even now. There was then and remains today only one gospel song to which we collectively knew all the words, and sang and danced to with abandon every Saturday night. It was "Movin' On Up," the theme to *The Jeffersons*.

As an adolescent in Shaker Heights, I tried to plot some middle ground between excelling like the white kids and being accepted—or at least left alone—by the black kids. At that time, there was no such Promised Land. So I conceived of my survival as a game: the Race Game. You pick up a card, a behavior or circumstance is described, you have to guess the race of the individuals involved. Sometimes I played for fun; sometimes I played as if my life depended upon it. White people often refer to the "race card," the excuse that blacks supposedly hold at the ready to explain away our failures. But for my generation, the first to embark upon the brave new world of integration, the Race Game was much more complex: an obstacle course, as intricate as chess, more exhausting than Monopoly.

Playing the game, I used my experience to guess not just who was what but how those people might think, feel, react. To hear the silent subtext, anticipate the racial insult that comes seemingly out of nowhere to hijack you, hold you back, put you in your place. Sometimes I still find myself playing it, though I also long for what is instinctive to my children: the freedom to take someone, anyone, at face value.

One day, in junior high school, I hear a group of students enter the school library—cursing, bellowing, cackling—and I don't even have to peek between the stacks to know: they are black. They won't linger here, but while they do, I stay hidden.

Years later, in my thirties, I am in a boutique on the Upper East Side of New York, and the well-heeled shop ladies are discussing some missing stock: ankle bracelets, cute erasers, kitschy stuff. I bristle, expecting an accusation. The owner senses this and explains with an indulgent laugh, "This time of year the girls from such-and-so academy come in and take things, a springtime ritual of the senior class." I don't have to wonder: These girls are white and rich. The offense that I had anticipated did not come, and the owner knew to explain the situation: move ahead one step. But because these girls are privileged and white, their crime will be dismissed as a prank: move one step back.

That incident recalled a family discussion about race in my own childhood, when my sisters, who were attending the Hathaway Brown School for Girls in the early 1970s, came home with a similar story. They were slightly breathless and impressed with the exploits of the white girls—their friends—who regularly shoplifted at local pharmacies. My parents, astonished by the idea that shoplifting was an amusing pastime and frightened that my sisters were impressed with it, launched into a harangue on how we could not—should never even *consider*—doing what they did. We were angry at their tirade, an anger that would magnify through the years as we attended schools with well-to-do whites only to be reminded that we did not have their privileges, their safety net, their freedom. Our parents would continue to insist, often at the point where we were our most daring or inventive, to take note of how differently things can be interpreted when color is involved—their message *aim high* always diluted by the warning *but don't forget that you're black*. It was enough to radicalize many black children like us into the very militancy that our opportunities were supposed to render moot.

This is the part of the game that feels like Russian roulette: participate, work hard, move up, but act too much like everyone else and you risk losing everything. My husband, who was also educated in private schools and colleges, tells me that in the corporation where he now works, black people do not feel they have the same latitude as their white co-workers to read the newspaper half the day or "work from home." He is ever mindful of the way standards may unexpectedly shift when it comes to him, to us.

When I met him in law school, he was an artful tactician of pleasantness, managing to get along with everyone—black or white, radical or conservative. But after years in the corporate world, I have seen him develop a rigid, potent suspicion and an impatience with the children's belief that they are no different from anyone else. When our son Spenser wanted to be in the same class as his best friend, Seth (who is white), with a teacher his father and I know to be a racist (though white parents think she is superb), I was astonished when his father exploded, "What works for Seth will not work for you!" Spenser appealed to me with tear-filled eyes.

"You must trust us," I sighed. "We know the score." By the end of the year, Spenser's encounters with the teacher at school were enough to make him glad he wasn't in her class. He came around to our way of seeing things. You cannot win the game with your eyes shut.

Of course, times are mostly better now, so are we wrong to pass down this sensitivity to our children—so ready, willing, and able to greet all with open arms? Am I, mired forever in racialized thinking, dragging Sam and Spenser down with me? If I am on the side of caution, do I err? Will we ever get beyond race if we don't stop making so much of it? Isn't there room for reckless idealism? If the Dominick of Sam's long-ago story had been white, I would have disapproved, but laughingly, part of me admiring the spirit— and envying the freedom—that it takes to be an irrepressible cutup. But because he was black, Dominick's bad behavior raised the ante and my antennae. I was less amused, more cautious, afraid for him and my sons and all the black boys who are too quickly discarded as trouble. As my parents had with me, I wanted Dominick to march boldly into the world, but not to take too many liberties, not to go too far.

I've decided that a rigid, unedifying color blindness cannot reign in my house. It is by taking note of race and all that accompanies it—the assumptions, the stereotypes flying to and fro like flaming arrows—that we can achieve a transcendental compassion, a unifying respect for the power of experience. People are people, there's no doubt about it, but you have to understand why things are the way they are. Not to take note of race or, more important, discuss it, would leave my sons in the dark. They must know where they stand and what to look out for, welcoming the surprise of those who reject the rules attached to skin color because to cleave to them would frustrate their inner truth. Luckily for my children, those rules are eroding, but they will endure if not consciously challenged.

Now twelve, Sam attends a summer camp for the academically gifted. He asks me, "Why are so many of these kids Asian and Indian?" The first time he asked, I ducked the question, not wanting to deal with all that it dredged up—the unpleasant racial competitiveness (*we* were here long before *them*), the bitterness of the black bourgeoisie toward blacks who, for myriad reasons, languish. But the second time he asked, I knew he wanted an answer, and why not? I have taught him to take note, and the exercise does not end with the observation. So I said, "In Asian and Indian cultures, learning has always been an activity for the elite and revered, and in America they know it is the key to upward mobility. For African American slaves, it could mean death, and until my generation, many blacks considered education worthless, since blacks were excluded from most gainful employment. Even today, higher education can have the effect of isolating many blacks from their community, leaving them to exist on the margins of a white society that is not yet fully inclusive." We talk and talk about the cultural differences, values, and attitudes that are inculcated over time and passed down to one generation from the next. And the talking continues.

The years since our conversation about the unruly Dominick have fermented deeper queries, ones that I also struggled with while growing up, playing the Race Game. Who does what and why? And, most critically: Where do I fit in?

The last question is the toughest to answer. Are you going to cling to the status quo, internalize the stereotypes and traditions? To be "truly black," will you avoid sushi, decline steak tartare? Or, because they symbolize the "non-black," dine on them until you are nauseated? To racially deny or neuter oneself, even to get ahead, exacts too high a price. I have searched for some compromise that embraces the reality of race but that challenges it too: one that leaves my children and me free to pursue a personal dimension but that sustains a keen political awareness of who we are, where we come from, and why.

I despised my parents for their mixed messages, the sleight of hand that always left us looking for the kernel of who we were under the shell of who we would never be. But now I appreciate that born of my parents' insistence on "white" things came a sense of new possibilities for me (proving, I suppose, the bromide that what doesn't kill you makes you stronger). Without their passionate, demanding myopia, I don't think I could have seen that I didn't have to wear the straightjacket of my color. Even as I sputtered and floundered in synchronized swimming and ran half-heartedly across the tennis court, I grew more confident in my determination that I didn't have to cast myself according to "script": to be a bump-dancing, loud-talking, finger-snapping black girl. If I could endure the unavoidable discomfort, the never fitting in or measuring up, I could go anyplace, learn anything, pick and choose from a constellation of behaviors and interests. I was free to explore my own way to becoming me.

My understanding of my parents, which grew with time and the forgiveness of one's parents that accompanies it, are gifts that

I hope Sam and Spenser will offer me. If I am wrong, and race doesn't matter to the extent that we should banish it forever from our conversation, I hope they'll understand why I thought it did. But for now, we routinely integrate race into our discussions. What I care about most is that these discussions are honest. Race doesn't determine the way my children see people—I am proud that they continue to give everyone a chance—but it is too potent to pretend it doesn't influence situations or alter lives. To grapple with it makes us better. My children and I don't always agree on what is racist, and they are free to say when the mere mention of the issue feels knee-jerk or unauthentic. When it is irresponsible not to discuss it, we face it together.

I have taught my children to note that other people—white or black—may think that being black means acting this way or that, but it doesn't have to mean that to them. I have exposed them to many things and have allowed them to embrace what they love. They have discovered that they prefer playing basketball to tennis or swimming, and that is fine with me.

I have dealt in the palindrome that race is involved in everything, but not everything is attributable to race. My theory is this: To realize how some people are likely to see you is an essential step to discovering and defending who you really are. I believe that I am, then, less a colonizer of my boys' impressionable minds than a tour guide to the world as it is, and it has been my job, in these formative years, to point out the major attractions, the time-wasting distractions, on the trip. Race is so many things along the way: a distorted fun-house mirror of misperception and depravity, a monument of cruelty and oppression. One must be familiar with the signposts of one's heritage—to measure the progress made, avoid the mistakes of the past, and ultimately, move to higher ground.

Berry covers a number of different time periods in the piece. It begins: "A few years ago…" in the past tense to describe the scene with her sons when race became an issue for them for the first time. But Berry makes it clear that she is writing from a "now" point of view. She ruminates in the present, tagging these ruminations with phrases like: "I wonder still..." and "Look, we all do it..."

Then Berry moves into her own past, into what shaped her: "My life has been..." This is a "diffused" past, because she is not focusing in on one moment in time; she is moving freely over years, back and then further back in time. But, like Jill Christman in "The Allergy Diaries," Berry doesn't let us forget that she is writing from a "now" perspective. She inserts herself here and there: "I suppose that is why..."; "Truthfully, I don't think..."; " ...though I also long for what is instinctive to my children: the freedom to take someone, anyone, at face value."

After Berry's dip into the past, she revisits the Dominick story, the incident that began her essay. She uses "I've decided" to make it clear that she has been mulling this over for years, trying to come to terms with it.

There are two scenes in the middle of this piece, however, where Berry shifts into straight immersion present tense: the junior high scene and the scene in the New York boutique. Perhaps she did this because those two memories particularly affected her. Regardless, we aren't left wondering where we are in time because she tags these paragraphs with "One day, in junior high" and "Years later."

The piece ends in the "now," when Berry is writing it, the "now" where Sam is 12. Her self-awareness, reflection, shifting perspective, and understanding of a moment and how she reacted to that moment are at the center of this piece. We need the history in order to fully understand her and her reaction to the Dominick story.

Think about the ways you incorporate the past and reflection into your writing. Backstory fleshes out our writing and makes it richer, but only include the past if it furthers the understanding of your current subject or characters. Always ask yourself: Does this help the reader understand me, what I've done, who I am?

WRITING EXERCISE: MEMORIES YOU MULL

It's clear that Berry had been mulling over not only the story of Dominick, but how race has affected her life and will affect her sons' lives. The thoughts, ideas, and memories that continue to pop into your mind are great fodder for writing. Make a list of experiences that you continue to think about long after the fact. Pick one and write for 20 minutes about how this has manifested in your life. How have you carried it (or not) into your life as a mother?

WRITING EXERCISE: WHAT DEFINES YOU?

Make a list of things that you feel have defined you. They could have to do with race or religion or politics or class, or even something like an alcoholic parent. Let your mind wander. After you have a list on paper, pick one of these defining things. Is there a turning point, a moment or scene that exemplifies the way this thing has defined you? Write for 15 minutes without stopping or censoring. See if you can get in touch with the details of a scene or moment. Then, free-write or list or cluster for another 15 minutes about how this thing manifests itself in your life as a parent. Have you had to confront it, come to terms with how it has worked in your life?

WRITING EXERCISE:
REFLECTION: THEN AND NOW

This is a slight variation of one of the voice exercises in Chapter 5. Think back to Sue William Silverman's description of how her voices of innocence and experience work together to allow her to reflect on her story. Make a list of the memorable events in your life (either before or after children). Pick one of these events and write it at the top of your page. Then make two columns, one titled "then" and one titled "now." Under the "then" column write the details as you remember them, including your reactions at the time and what sense you were making of what was happening. Under the "now" column write your more distanced reactions and thoughts. How do you see this event in your life now? For instance, if I were going to write about Stella's birth and hospitalization, under "then" I would list all my fears and the anger and frustration I felt at not having things turn out as I hoped they would. Under the "now" column I might write about how lucky I realize we were that she made it to 32 weeks. I might also list the ways my outlook on life changed because of our experiences in the NICU and after.

❧❧❧

CHAPTER 10

OUR PARENTING PARTNERS

A COUPLE OF YEARS AFTER WE WERE MARRIED, Donny took a poetry class at The Loft, our local literary center, and at the end of the semester there was a public reading where students read what they'd written over the course of the class. I sat in the crowded classroom as my husband stood up and read a poem about *me*. I knew he was going to do this; he'd asked my permission. I quickly granted it; after all, I wrote about him all the time so it was only fair. But as soon as he opened his mouth to read, I felt my face flush, the heat traveling down my neck and spreading across my shoulders. It was a poem about how I had struggled with depression, and how helpless he felt when I became crippled by anxiety. *Oh shit,* I thought. *So this is what it feels like to have someone write about you.* I felt exposed and vulnerable. Even though I had covered these very topics in my own writing, it was different coming from him: they weren't my words; I wasn't in control.

It was an important lesson for me as a memoirist, especially as a memoirist who writes about my husband and our relationship. Every writer of creative nonfiction needs to decide how she will deal with this issue. When you're just beginning to work on something new (whether it is an essay or a whole book), it's best to pretend that no one is going to read it—ever. If you're worried about what the people you are writing about will think, you'll self-censor and may skirt around the heart of the piece. But when you are ready to send your writing into the world—whether it's on a blog, at a reading, in a literary journal, or in a book—you need to take some time thinking about how what you've written will affect the people about whom you've written.

I know some writers who write what they feel they need to write, publish it, and *then* talk to their families about it. This is not my approach. I try to write what I need to write and let my people read it before I publish it. If you are truthful and really spend time making your characters three-dimensional, most people are very forgiving (and even honored) that you have written about them.

After I had finished a full draft of my memoir, I knew I had to let my mom read it, and I was really nervous because I wrote some things about her that I knew would hurt her feelings. I printed out the manuscript and handed it to her with a caveat. I said, "Mom, I know I was a brat in some of these scenes. But I tried to present everything as honestly as I could."

She read it and told me she loved it and then said, "You're right, you were a brat in some places, but that's how it happened." I was so relieved, and I think her reading what I wrote actually made us closer. It took me a while to get to this place with the writing, though. A reader of an early draft of the book said, "I'm not getting a sense of your mom. I feel there is more there, between you, but we don't yet know what it is." I didn't really want to write some of those scenes, but I needed to do it in order to make the book emotionally truthful and to really honor my relationship with my mom. (When she read these very paragraphs, she wrote in the margin, "But you're such a sweet and honest brat! Love you!" Thanks, Mom!)

Whenever I'm writing about people in my life, I try to be respectful and then trust my instincts. In "To Fashion a Text," Annie Dillard says, "I don't believe in a writer's kicking around people who don't have access to a printing press. They can't defend themselves." If you feel you've kicked someone around in your writing, maybe you need to revisit those passages and ask yourself whether you've presented this person as three-dimensional. I also think it's helpful to really question whether a certain portrayal or character is necessary for the story you're telling. If it's not, maybe you don't need to include it in your story.

When I write about Donny, I let him read everything. He is my biggest supporter—he has held me when I wept about rejection letters, he has told me I'm a wonderful writer when I didn't believe it, and we have lived together under a shadow of financial insecurity for years so I can follow my dream—writing and teaching. I wouldn't do anything to "kick him around." He is also very gracious about what I choose to write about—his childhood with a schizophrenic mother, our disagreements and irritations, even arguments. There is only one scene in my memoir with which he disagreed. "I wouldn't have said that. I didn't say that," he said. "But that's how I remember it," I countered. "But that's not how it happened," he insisted. It was a small thing, really, and it didn't affect the emotional truth of the scene, so I changed it. It was the least I could do. And recently, when he read the latest version of the book, I kept checking in with him—is that how you remember it? Is everything that I've written OK with you? Yes and yes.

One of the things I try to do in my writing is turn that critical lens on myself. If I am really examining my actions and motives and not letting myself off the hook, I think it is easier for others to swallow scenes where I turn a critical lens on them. All of your characters—including yourself—need to be three-dimensional.

In Chapter 4 on character development, I mentioned how it's sometimes challenging to write about the people to whom we are closest because we take their gestures and faces and body language for granted. We are so close to them that it is difficult to see them clearly. This is certainly true of our spouses and partners. In order to get Donny down on the page as a three-dimensional character in my memoir, I had to actually "study" him; I watched how he held his hands and head, how his lips pursed when he was angry. Then I was able to include all of these details in the memoir.

We are going to return to character development in this chapter and focus our gaze (with everything we have learned about craft so far) on our spouses and parenting partners. If you are single mother, you might choose to focus on the lack of a parenting partner in your life or turn your gaze to others who help parent your children, whether this is another family member, a child-care provider, or a friend.

The stories we're writing are never just about our children, as you've seen in the pieces in this book and I'm sure in your own writing. Our stories are about us as parents and people; they are about shifts in perspective, about finding a new lens through which to see the world; they are about grief and letting go.

Becoming a parent changes our relationships with our partners in so many ways, and this is one of the reasons that writing about our partners is such an important part of writing about motherhood.

As we write our partners into our stories, it's helpful to get the essence of him or her down on paper in as much detail as possible. Here is an example of that from Beth Kephart's *A Slant of Sun*, a memoir about Kephart discovering that her son Jeremy (from "The Line Is Narrow and It Is White") has a Pervasive Developmental Disorder, Not Otherwise Specified—an autism spectrum disorder. One of the things I like most about this book is how Kephart writes about herself and her husband, Bill.

In the chapter "Reaching for My Son," Kephart writes:

[My husband] inhabits his soul with more ease than I do mine, and time does not defeat him: there will be, he predicts, another day. Patient, he waits. An artist, he disdains calculations, expectations, routine, and he is in and out of space and language—prone to laughing, out of the blue, at a joke his brother made, not today or even last week, but decades ago, in El Salvador, at the water hole on the coffee farm beneath a cliff of yellow parrots. He paints and makes the old man young or the plaster bleed or the priest name his assassin, and when my husband makes his guitar sing, he falls deep inside old Spanish, closes his eyes, and finds himself where he wants to be: among the swollen smells of orange rinds and steamed *pupusas*, above the slow creak of a cotton hammock, near the familiar noise of the domestic help snapping spiders out of bedsheets. My husband is at home inside himself—leaving the things he can't control to the gods, and content with all the rest. It is this easiness of manner that gives those who know him strength.

I am the opposite, all celerity and hurry, approaching each day with the assailing, urgent sense that time is passing, that days are numbered, that the beasts of possibility must be unleashed. I have my father's habits, rising long before dawn, and I prowl the house the way insomniacs do, ticking tasks off in my mind, arranging incongruous responsibilities, hefting pegs into an imaginary board. Walking from room to room in the dark, I pull the drapes aside, separate the white slats of the blinds, and check the neighbors' houses for a beacon, a sign that I am not the lone vigilante of the night. Pacing the narrow, lusterless floorboards, navigating furniture and toys, abandoned coffee mugs, dust on shelves, I make lists while others sleep, and finally I settle into my desk, a rectangle of teak on two firm trestles that moors me and saves me. There I sit before the window that I've never dressed and watch the night give in to day, the pink bursting through the Prussian blue before flattening itself to gold.

Who we are and how we inhabit the world affects every aspect of our lives, including parenthood. We come away from these paragraphs with a sense of who Beth and Bill are as people, which is important for the book, because we need to understand their different approaches to parenting their son. Read these paragraphs aloud and notice how Kephart's tone shifts when she moves from writing about her husband to writing about herself. In the paragraph about her husband, her language is slow, relaxed, luscious. In the paragraph where she describes herself, her sentences feel rushed, reflecting exactly how she is describing herself: "all celerity and hurry."

As your partners appear in your pages of writing, consider these questions: How do we know him or her? How would you describe his or her voice? What do we know about your relationship and what do we know about how the two of you work together as parents?

It's important for the reader to know you and your partner so that when something changes—whether it is the birth of a new child, an illness, or a worry—the reader can understand how this change or challenge is not only affecting you, the narrator, but also the other parent. We need to know how this change affects your relationship. If you are writing about a challenge or crisis with one of your children, part of the story might also be how you and your partner deal with these challenges differently or the same way. Navigating this changing relationship is often part of the larger story.

WRITING EXERCISE:
WRITING YOUR PARTNER

This exercise is similar to the character sketch exercise from Chapter 4, this time focusing on your partner. Don't worry about writing a scene or even a paragraph. I just want you to make a list. Think of your partner's essence: how does he talk? How does she hold herself? What does he wear? What does he look like when he's irritated? What does she look like just before she gets angry? Think about physical appearance, gesture, dialogue. How does he phrase things? What is his favorite word? Get as much down in a list or paragraph form as you can.

Then read what you've written. Have you captured your partner's essence on the page? Have you captured his personality? What details did you omit? What details could be misleading? Go back to your list and add or flesh out certain characteristics. I want you to be able to say: he is this, he is that. This list might not appear in your writing in a paragraph as it did in the excerpt from *A Slant of Sun*. But maybe you will incorporate this information into your writing with a line here and a line there.

Having a clear sense of this person as you're writing will help you get your partner onto the page. The following scene is from a memoir-in-progress by a former student, Marilyn Bousquin. The stage of the memoir is when Bousquin's son is a teenager, a time when the demands of motherhood catapult her back to the Catholicism of her childhood. But in the process of writing, Bousquin discovered the ways that parenting had strained her relationship with her husband even when their son was an infant. "At the time, I didn't realize the strain as an offshoot of parenting," she says, "but the writing process revealed tensions in our relationship that intensified when we became parents." The scene below illustrates how personal coping mechanisms within the dynamics of a relationship can aggravate the stress of parenting. "Writing honestly about my own shortcomings as a mother," Bousquin says, "surprised me with the gift of self-awareness and insights into my relationship with my husband."

From Marilyn's memoir-in-progress:

Sam, two months old, was asleep in his bouncer on the counter of our tiny apartment when I received the package from my mother. She loved sending "happiness" presents. "Keep a look-see for a little something in the mail," she'd say. But this package, a rectangular box wrapped in brown paper cut from a grocery bag, arrived without warning in today's mail.

The paper crinkled as I opened it, and Sam, who'd been napping for hours, rooted in his sleep. Milk seeped through my bra and T-shirt. Sometimes I would wake in the night to milk leakage seconds before he cried for a feeding, my body intuiting his needs.

"He's hungry," I said to Steve, who was reading in the fake-leather recliner across the apartment. He put his book down and joined me at the counter while I opened the package.

The torn paper revealed a white box, slightly yellowed, and when I lifted its lid a faint attic smell emerged. I pulled a bustle of white fabric and a matching bonnet from wads of yellowed, waxy tissue paper.

"She sent him a dress?" Steve asked. He was raised a Southern Methodist and did not register the bustle of white tulle and taffeta, cotton and lace, as a baptismal gown. I recognized it as more than a baptismal gown. It was a jab under the rib, my mother's judgment of my lapse of Catholicism, which felt, in this context, like a judgment of me as a mother.

"Damn her!" I yelled, throwing the gown into the box. Sam's eyes opened, his face gathered. He let out a howl.

Steve stiffened, then reached for the baby. I tried to reach past him, to gather Sam, whom I knew I'd just frightened, but Steve edged me away with his elbow and lifted Sam, who was shrieking now, full-belly wails, to his chest.

"Sshhh," Steve said, rubbing his back. "It's okay. There now. Sshhh." Steve turned away from me and walked across the room.

My milk ducts pulled, and I cupped my breasts.

Three years ago, when my mother said that if we didn't get married in the Catholic Church she wouldn't attend our wedding, Steve had comforted me as I raged, then cried. His calm and my expressiveness had drawn us together, a tender balance. Since Sam was born, these traits that once kept us in tandem seemed to drive us apart. The louder I yelled, the further Steve retreated into silence. I sometimes wondered if we were the same two people who'd created this child.

My breasts felt suddenly engorged. I followed Steve across the apartment and reached for my howling baby, but again Steve turned his back to me, making his way to the recliner. I knew he was mad and that his edging me out was an attempt to protect and comfort his son without being overtly mean to me, but my entire body ached to nurse Sam, to comfort him myself.

"I'm sorry," I said. Since Sam's birth, it seemed my expressiveness was more akin to the knee-jerk temper I'd had as a kid, or was I just more aware of it now that my outbursts frightened my son? Yet I couldn't seem to stop myself. "But she did that on purpose. That's her way of telling me to have him baptized. Damn her." Sam had quieted, was rooting on Steve's shoulder, bobbing his head, trailing saliva. My breasts ached.

Steve looked at me, his eyes tired. I knew he was thinking *Don't do that again*. I was not proud of my tendency to overreact, but Steve's habit of withdrawing, his impenetrableness, left me feeling disconnected, alone. Part of me wanted us to duke it out with an old-fashioned fistfight that would leave us breathless but clinging to each other, our frustrations spent.

"He's hungry," he said.

"I know."

He handed Sam to me. I took a deep breath, inhaling Sam's baby smell. "I'm sorry," I whispered into his head, "Mommy scared you."

I sat in the wooden rocker across the room, lifted my soggy T-shirt, and unclipped a cup of my nursing bra. Sam latched on to my nipple, and I rocked gently as he suckled and my breast eased. Steve picked up his book, resumed reading.

The first night of his life, Sam had wailed full throttle for hours. I cuddled him, nursed him, changed him, burped him, until finally, uncertain about what he needed, what I should do, I let him wail, holding him close. In the cot next to my hospital bed, the empty bassinet between us, Steve snored loudly. When Sam finally slept, not only did I feel the deep ache of exhaustion, stitches smarting my torn perineum, but I also heard in Steve's snore an obliviousness to Sam's needs, to my needs, as if he were snoring on purpose, and I resented him. Yet at the same time, I wanted to talk to him. Our relationship was built on marathon conversations, and I wanted the comfort of his voice on that first night of our baby's life. I wondered as I lay there awake, Sam curled into the crook of my arm, hospital sounds beeping, Steve snoring, if we would ever talk again.

Steve turned a page of his book. We were all quiet now, me nursing, Sam suckling, Steve reading. The baptismal gown lay limp on the counter. I rocked Sam in the wooden rocker, the same chair my mother had rocked me in, its spindles stained with breast milk. When I switched him to my other breast, he latched on with gusto, sweat pearling his head.

"He's doing his sweat thing," I said to Steve. We both loved the way Sam sweated when he nursed. He sweated when he slept, too, and sometimes we just watched him sweat and sleep.

"He sure loves to eat," he said, lowering his book, leaning forward.

I nodded and rocked, lowering my nose, my lips, to his bald, sweaty head.

Bousquin's scene illustrates how even when we are in the same room with our spouse, we can feel apart, isolated. So often we experience the same events in such different ways. Who we are plays a role in that. I remember those early stressful months with Stella, and how our worries, coupled with intense exhaustion, made Donny and me shadows of our former, loving selves. We handed the baby back and forth, took turns sleeping, and that was about it. Our emotional distance was further strain on our relationship, and it took time to reestablish the closeness and playfulness between us.

WRITING EXERCISE: PARENTING STRAIN

Have there been certain times in your life as a parent when you and your partner particularly struggled? The stressful times could be due to a crisis or illness with one of your children, or to other external forces: the economy, complicated relationships with your families of origin. Pick one time when you and your partner were not seeing eye to eye or when your personality traits seemed to work against each other. Write a scene from that time in as much detail as possible, as Bousquin did above. How did you end up making it past that? Did you?

WRITING EXERCISE:
NAVIGATING RELATIONSHIP CHANGES

How did having children change your relationship with your spouse or partner? You can just make a list. Is there something on your list that calls out for further writing? Free-write about that. How have you managed to navigate these changes?

WRITING EXERCISE: PARENTING STYLES

How does your spouse or partner interact with your children differently than you do? Make a list. Be as detailed as you can. Does this create tension in your relationship, or has it in the past? Describe it in as much detail as possible.

CHAPTER 11

STRUCTURE:
HOW TO PUT IT TOGETHER

WHEN I BEGAN WRITING MY MEMOIR, I TRIED NOT to think about the fact that I was writing a book. It was too daunting, too huge. I simply took my laptop to the coffee shop near my house and "vomited" all the images and moments and memories and thoughts about my pregnancy and Stella's birth and her hospitalization onto the computer. I didn't worry about form or structure or how these snippets would fit together. But after several months and about 45 single-spaced pages, I realized that my "vomit" had a shape. (Sorry, that sounds gross.) The paragraphs began to fall into three categories: pregnancy, NICU, and home. So I began to rearrange sections of the book until they were basically in chronological order. This is still the structure of my memoir—it's a chronological story fleshed out with backstory.

The biggest challenge in terms of structure came in the revision process, as I was trying to figure out when the reader needed certain pieces of backstory. Originally I had a whole chapter of backstory about my relationship with Donny and our desire for children. I also had a whole chapter about my worries concerning mental illness. Both of these long, drawn-out backstory chapters slowed the narrative down to a point of stalling it. (It wasn't me who realized this, of course; it was my insightful agent.) After she pointed it out, I went back to the question: *What is the heart of my story?* I sat with that question for a while and eventually decided that if the book is about learning to live with uncertainty and about the power of stories to connect us, I didn't really need all that backstory. So I condensed three full chapters of backstory into a few paragraphs here and a few paragraphs there. The book is much tighter as a result.

Sometimes the structure of a piece arises organically, and it seems that the piece chooses how it wants to be structured; other times, it might take multiple drafts and many attempts at different structures to find the one that fits, the one that best serves the piece of writing. Structure is always tied to the story, and identifying the heart of your piece will help you decide what kind of structure you need.

A few years ago I was working on a short piece for the online journal *Brevity*. It was a piece about time I spent living in a small village in Costa Rica, and I thought it was an essay about race and difference. I originally structured the piece in five numbered sections. But I realized that the numbers weren't doing enough work, so I thought about what I was really saying and whether there was another way to title the sections that would better hold the piece together. It was only when I realized that the piece was about belonging and culture that I understood how to connect the sections. I ended up organizing the piece based on the stages of moving through culture shock; each section is titled with one of these stages. I needed that understanding of the story before the structure made sense.

Structure can also reflect a narrator's state of mind. In Chapter 5, I discussed the importance of voice in reflecting the emotional context of a scene (as in "The Allergy Diaries," when Jill and Mark are panicking during Ella's allergic reaction). Structure can do this, as well. A great example of this is Debra Gwartney's *Live Through This*, a memoir about Gwartney's two teenage daughters running away. There are sections of this memoir that circle around themselves. For instance, Gwartney might be narrating a scene, then back up and explain what led up to that scene. Then she's back in the scene, then forward in time, past the events of the scene. This circular structure heightens the disorientation and the just-getting-by feeling that Gwartney was experiencing at that point in her life. When I interviewed her, I asked her whether the book's structure was a conscious choice or whether that was simply how the narrative emerged. This is what she said:

While writing the book, I relished the idea of suspending time. For me, the layering of events, no matter the month or year those events took place, helped establish the patterns that eventually led to our troubles. Sven Birkerts writes about this kind of structuring in his marvelous book *Art of Time in Memoir*, and cautions (wisely I think) against the tendency to get episodic, *this happened, and then this happened, and then this...*

I was much more interested in delving into symbols, metaphors, and lyricism than adhering to chronology, and I tended to pick up on a detail—putting the tent up in our living room, or standing in the rain in the downtown square confronting my daughters, or eating at a Chinese food restaurant with [my older daughter]—and let my writerly mind make intuitive connections with other times, other episodes. So it was a swirl—the disorientation of that period in my family life, but also the recognition of the nature of your heart and mind when you're trying to sort out your life, or a significant portion of your life. All kinds of information and memories, and from many different times, pour in as you strive to understand how you got to this point, to this place. At least that's how the process worked for me, and I wanted the writing to express that somehow. My editor wisely convinced me to make the narrative more straightforward, less discombobulated, and I soon agreed that was the way to go. Still, the narrative isn't linear, and I hope I was able to express the

encounters with time, images, and emotions as I began to recon-
cile the past with the present.

The fact that the structure of your writing can express your emotional
state is such an exciting idea, and it can be freeing as you're trying to
figure out the best way to construct an essay or memoir. It's important
also to trust your gut when it comes to structure. I tried to change the
beginning of my memoir several times, but I kept returning to the initial
chapter—it was just where my gut was telling me the book began.

This reminds me of something author Vicki Forman said when I
asked her how she came to the structure of her memoir, *This Lovely
Life*. This book is about the extremely premature birth of Forman's
twins, one of whom dies just days after birth. The first chapter is very
long and moves back and forward in time, beginning with a reflection
on grief, then moving to the birth of the twins, forward to the days
following the birth, backward to the night of the birth, and forward
again. Throughout, she gives lines and paragraphs of backstory as well,
and the chapter ends with her daughter's death.

When I asked Vicki about this chapter, she said:

I always knew the first chapter had to be long because I wanted to
tell in one long moment the entirety of our first four days as the
parents of very premature babies: the shocking, sudden premature birth, the realization that the twins would be resuscitated,
the rush to the NICU after their birth and the difficult decision,
not 48 hours later, to remove our daughter from life support. I
kept thinking of the opening segment of *Goodfellas*, and how
Scorsese uses one very long opening sequence to set the tone for
the whole movie. For me, I wanted the book to begin that way,
to have every pertinent element of the entire story incorporated
into the opening. But as I contemplated how to do this, I also
realized the opening would have to be very long if I was going
to cover those whole four days, and the entirety of that experi-

ence. And this was a struggle for me because I worried about keeping the reader's interest throughout what was essentially a 40-page opening sequence. Most books on craft would tell you that's probably far too long an opening. I tried breaking it up over and over, with different kinds of cuts, shorter chapters, you name it, and I just kept coming back to the idea that the beginning of the book was meant to be a very long first movement, and that when it was over, if I'd done my job well, the reader would feel entirely submerged into the experience in the same way I had been submerged. This was one of those decisions, as a writer, where I felt I had to go with my instincts even if another writer might have considered a different option. We can think about craft as abstractly and for as long as we like, but honestly it's intuition that guides us all, eventually.

In Chapter 2, I quoted Patricia Hampl, who said that a first draft "hasn't yet found its subject; it isn't yet about what it wants to be about." To echo that sentiment, sometimes we end up fighting against the structures that our pieces need. But as Forman said, we need to give ourselves permission to let our writing be structured the way it wants to be structured. And her first chapter does, indeed, make the reader "feel entirely submerged into the experience," just as she hoped.

In this book we've read linear pieces like Kephart's "The Line Is White, and It Is Narrow" and pieces with a tight frame, where most of the action takes place in backstory, such as Divakaruni's "Common Scents" and Sara Martin's "Music in His Genes." We've read pieces that employ a diffused past, such as Berry's "Was He Black or White?" We've read present-tense pieces and past-tense pieces. In this chapter, I will be discussing sectioned and collage structures in two short essays.

SECTIONING

As you read the following essay, Anne Greenwood Brown's "Insights," consider what effect the short, titled sections have on the piece.

Insights

· ·

The Trick

Here's the trick. I am pressing the end of a flashlight against my pregnant belly. I press the switch, and the light glows like fire through my taut flesh, making it look like an enormous blood orange. I am ripe with expectations. My husband waits patiently, his hand pressed against my side, waiting for the baby to kick. But the baby isn't impressed with the intrusion, finds no offense in the light, and the trick doesn't work. My husband makes some comment that this baby is coy. He takes the flashlight from me, turns it off, and drops it on the floor.

We lie awake in the dark, whispering our dreams, directing our baby's future. We run through our short list of names. We predict a future president. By the time I fall asleep, a small smile still clinging to my lips, I have written the script for our baby's life.

Ad Libbing

The thing about scripts is the actors forget their lines, props go missing, sets tip over. Occasionally someone takes a sandbag to the head. When Sophie is born, the lights go out. Twenty-four-hours old, and a pediatric ophthalmologist is talking about calcification and retinal tears. When my husband asks if she will need glasses right away, the doctor says, "She'll never read print or drive a car." Some doctors are assholes. And our daughter is blind.

Losing It

My mother says, "You write all day long. Why don't you write about this?" But there are no words. My ears are full of sound. My mind is numb. I squeeze my eyes so tight I fear they will turn inside out. I sit on the bathtub drain and turn on the shower so no one can hear me crying. I can't write about this because I am ashamed, and to write about shame is a confession of guilt. My two older children are busy drawing pictures. They tape them to the wall by the crib. "They are for Sophie," they say. "She will like the colors." And I can't tell them that it doesn't matter. That the baby can't see their pictures. And I am ashamed I can't tell them the truth: I have made something less than perfect. I worry my husband blames me, though he'd never say it. Did I have too much caffeine? Forget my vitamins? Sleep on the wrong side? But the guilt is nothing compared to pity. Pity comes like a wave that washes over me and sucks me down until I don't know which way is up. I agonize that she will never see my face, never know the look in my eyes that says I love her. She will never stand on stage and see me waving to her from the audience. I worry she will never have any friends. The loss of everything I have dreamt for her has left me gasping for air.

Faking It

Two years later and I am carving out some strange, new definition of normal. It is normal for a toddler to be quiet. It is normal for a toddler to be still. But then we step outside, and every other two-year-old reminds me of what should have been. When Sophie faces the world, her eyes are small and sunken. Her eye sockets are purple pools. While the other toddlers climb over the monkey bars, my biceps burn from carrying a child who should have been walking a year ago. It makes it so much harder to pretend. I speak brave words to the other mothers and wave off their concerned looks with the back of my hand. "Blindness. It is nothing." But even now, it only takes a stranger's sideways look to crack the facade. A five-year-old walks over to our picnic blanket. She has the audacity to crouch down and stare into my child's vacant eyes. I attack the curious girl with words too shameful to repeat. She is frightened, and I see the reflection of a crazy woman in her wide eyes. Air catches in my throat, and I fake a smile. "No, no, no. So sorry. See? Everything's okay. Nothing to worry about." But she runs away to her mother and points at us. I pack our things and go back home.

Waking Words

Sophie is listening. She is building a vocabulary and memorizing patterns, studying cadence and texture, without ever letting on. When she wakes one morning, after thirty months of silence, she opens her mouth and speaks in eloquent, lilting sentences that echo my grandmother's formal style.

"How lovely to see you," she says. I am dumbstruck. Sophie continues to string together words like a lifeline, and I feel myself being pulled up and out of the hole I have so foolishly created and into Sophie's world—a world of delicate sensitivities more beautiful than the conspicuous world in which I live.

Lessons in Listening

One month later and I am lifting Sophie from her high chair.

"What is a heliotrope?" she asks.

There is no lisp. Every syllable is distinct. I don't know the answer, but she doesn't mind. "It feels nice on my tongue," she says. I roll the word around a few times myself and agree. I run a warm bath and she slides in. The suds build into frothy mountains.

"Why are you giggling?" I ask as I run the washcloth over her back.

"Shh," she says.

I close my eyes so I can hear what I am missing. Microscopic soap bubbles are bursting in a fine fizzing along the edge of the tub. It is like the static on the power lines in the middle of a Minnesota winter. I keep my eyes closed to discover just a little more. The water is warm, and it slips up my arm like an elegant glove.

Sophie laughs and rolls inelegantly in the water, like a seal in the surf.

Later that night, I read to her and she is smiling. "Do you like this story?" I ask.

"Yes, but who is whispering?"

"Is somebody whispering?"

"They're saying, 'shwoop...shwoop...shwoop.' But now they've stopped." We listen for a while, but there is no one there.

I turn the page with a soft shuffle of paper, and Sophie announces, "They're back."

Words of Reconciliation

Words are magic. They can puncture your heart and throw you into despair. But they can just as easily heal and make bridges where none existed before. Sophie's observations on the world, and the words she uses to capture them, are a balm to my ragged heart. We lie together in the yard, and she tells me what she knows. I capture it all in a notebook. Grass is a brutal offense and deserving of the word blade. Sophie refuses to walk barefoot across it. To bite into an apple sounds like an assault, which she refuses to commit.

I draw a veil over those early days. I press my face into Sophie's hair and inhale deeply. There is nothing but happiness in this child, and she is taking me with her.

This story—Greenwood Brown learning to see the beauty in her daughter—could be told in a book-length memoir, but here she does it in seven short sections. Each section is a snapshot that moves us through Greenwood Brown's acceptance of Sophie's blindness and into her appreciation and love for her daughter, to the place where Sophie's words about the world are a balm to her mother's "ragged heart."

Instead of writing a whole chapter on getting the diagnosis of Sophie's blindness, Greenwood Brown writes, "Twenty-four-hours old, and a pediatric ophthalmologist is talking about calcification and retinal tears." That is all we need to know for this piece. More writing at that point would have bogged down the narrative.

Sometimes your story can be more powerful when you focus on the critical moments in short sections, as Greenwood Brown does. But writing your story in a shorter form can also help you clarify the necessary scenes or moments that need to be in a longer version. Or conversely, you can chisel away at a bigger story until you have what you feel is its essence, and this can be powerful as its own short piece *and* helpful in defining what your bigger story actually is.

WRITING EXERCISE:
FROM LONG TO SHORT IN SECTIONS

Think of a piece you'd like to write or that you've already written in a longer form. Instead of telling the story in fleshed-out scenes and paragraphs of reflection, what would happen if you told your story in five or six titled sections? What are the main themes you'd like to get across? Which scenes or moments or reflections can hold your story? Think of this in terms of snapshots.

COLLAGE

Though Greenwood Brown's "Insights" is organized in chronological order, its snapshot sections are collage-like and let us see and understand the author's heartbreak, acceptance, then admiration for the special gifts that Sophie possesses.

Collage can also allow a writer to paste together seemingly disconnected bits of writing to create meaning. What happens when you take one or two or three different pieces of writing and splice them together? Sometimes this can open up the possibilities in a piece and help push your writing to a deeper, more metaphorical level. What effect do the two narrative threads have in the following piece by Lisa Kahn Schnell?

Circling
Daffiama, Ghana
· ·

I.

There was a woman who died while I was in Daffiama; she was young and eight months pregnant. I didn't go to the funeral, but those who did said you could see the baby circling around inside of her, like a hand moving under a sheet. Later I felt bad that I hadn't gone to the funeral, but I was never sure if my motivation was guilt or disappointment over missing such a spectacle.

II.

My own babies have died inside me twice now. The first one fell with the Twin Towers, and as the clots of blood dripped into the toilet, I said goodbye almost thankfully, glad not to bring a child into such a world. This one is taking its time, and I have nothing more than my intuition to tell me that it's gone.

III.

I am haunted by this scene: the woman, the funeral, the baby circling around. They cut the baby out in order to bury her, but only after it had stopped circling and had died. I didn't go to the funeral—my fiancé was visiting, and I didn't know the woman. But I should have gone. I should have gone not just to support the family, and not just because you never know when it's going to be your turn to grieve or be grieved, but because knowing what I know now about my own life, I see that there are things I would have learned, maybe things I would have taken from that funeral if I had the courage.

IV.

This time nothing is falling: no blood, no towers, I just know. Something is different, something has changed, and I search my body for signs that my baby is still there—check my breasts, my belly, the fluid in the toilet, and back again to the breasts, wondering if the life inside me has died. I'm still not completely sure, so I survey again, trying to find the feeling that was once there, that still comes back in little wisps, but seems mostly gone. There is something about the way the breasts suddenly deflate, the way the body stops gurgling and humming, that lets me know I will continue to chase after the symptoms of another life in my body without ever finding what I am looking for.

V.

I am the color brown. Not just any brown, but the kind you make with paint or too many layers of crayon when you're a little kid. You mix all the colors together—the good colors and the bad colors too, just to see what will happen, and you come up with a muddy, greenish, sickly version of the color brown, a sort of chaos and confusion of life and lifelessness all blended into one, never to be separated into sky blue, tangerine, and sea foam again. This brown, this color I am, it sucks in the colors of crocuses, bananas, my husband's eyes, and it holds them tight, keeping them for its own but never changing, never brightening to a rich mahogany or surrendering to black. That is what color I am right now.

VI.

If I knew then what I know now, what would I have done? I would have gone to the funeral and made them cut the baby out while it was still alive, instead of after it had died. I would have taken the dead woman's baby for my own, as a guard against the possibility that either of us would ever be alone, as a stone thrown in the face of death, as protection against this circling, this looking for something we both need desperately that is no longer there.

Kahn Schnell alternates telling the story of the woman and baby in Daffiama with her own story of her miscarriages. The thing that connects these two threads is loss. The only section that departs from this structure is section V, where the author describes being the color brown. This is where she steps out of the two threads and describes her emotional state.

One of my students said, "I love the title; it describes not only this mythical baby circling in the dead mother's womb, but also the author's thoughts, going around and around that dead baby and her own two miscarriages. This format is effective here because this is how our minds work—we go back and forth from memory to the here and now to imagining the future and back again, revising the past in our minds." Kahn Schnell's title helps readers make these connections as they read her piece.

WRITING EXERCISE:
TWO THREADS

Make a list of at least 10 things that circle around in your mind. They could be memories or stories you've heard—things that have a hold on your imagination. Choose one and write three short paragraphs, which can be connected or not. Then choose another topic from your list and do the same. Then splice them together. What happens to your piece?

You may choose to let this sit for a few days, and then come back to it and see what connections you can make between the two threads. Do they speak to each other? What is the real story underneath and between them? Do they inform each other? Rewrite both threads with this new understanding in mind.

CHAPTER 12

RE-VISIONING YOUR WRITING

IN CHAPTER 5 I MENTIONED THAT WHEN MY MEMOIR was first shopped around to editors in 2007, it was rejected (and rejected and rejected and rejected.) It wasn't a fun year, but—and this is something I never thought I'd say—I'm grateful that it *was* rejected.

Many of the editors claimed there was no market for "preemie memoirs." Others wanted the book to be funnier or edgier. And even though I didn't put much stock in these responses, on some level I knew the book wasn't as good as it could be. So I asked my agent to stop sending it out, and that is when I began rewriting the book.

And by rewriting I really mean re-writing, writing it again. I printed out all 307 pages of my manuscript. Then I opened a new, blank document on my computer and began to retype my memoir from the beginning, keeping in mind my understanding of what the book is really about.

I didn't retype it word for word. I followed the same basic plotline, and I kept a few sentences here and there exactly the same, but for the most part I actually wrote the book again, using the printed draft as a guide. If I were just cutting and pasting and tweaking sentences, it would have been more difficult to actually see the material in a new way.

It took me over two and a half years, but it was worth it; the book is so much better than it was. Because the page was blank, I was freer to move in new directions. I was really able to see it with new eyes. And the writing skills I had gained in the intervening years made their way onto the page in ways I didn't expect. I had a more intuitive sense about when I needed to linger in scene and when I needed more reflection.

So much of the work of a writer takes place in the revision process. (I can't count the number of times I've heard "writing is revising.") But I think it's often helpful and important to write a full draft before you begin mucking around in your manuscript too much.

BIG-PICTURE REVISION

When you are ready to revise, it's helpful to think about revision on two levels. There is big-picture revision, where you ask *What is the story?* and *What does this piece really want to be?* in an effort to get at the heart of the story, to tease it out of the shadows if necessary.

When I realized that my memoir was not only about learning to live with uncertainty, but also about the power of words and stories to connect us to one another, I knew I needed to make sure those themes were pulled through the whole narrative. You don't want your major themes or metaphors to suddenly disappear from your story—you want them to remain in the readers' minds as they are reading. That may mean revisiting them throughout the narrative. When I was in graduate school, I took a class with Patricia Hampl in which she described this process in terms of sewing. She said to imagine yourself sewing your narrative. When you need to revisit a theme, imagine you are reaching down and taking a stitch. How many stitches you need is going to depend on your story; just make sure you haven't abandoned one of your narrative threads.

REVISING CRAFT

The other level in revision focuses on craft: Are your scenes working as hard as they can? Do you need to tweak dialogue? Add more dialogue? Cut dialogue that's not working? Have you developed a clear sense of place and time in your piece? Do you have enough reflection? Is your voice consistent throughout the piece? Does it ring true?

Revising craft involves taking everything you have learned about creative nonfiction and making sure you've applied it in your writing. You take what you've already written and make it better. This is the kind of revision that makes your writing sing. Look at your characters. Have you fully developed them on the page? Revisit your scenes and decide which ones need to be fleshed out and which ones might be better as a couple of lines of summary. Other questions to ask yourself as you revise:

- How does the reader know me as the narrator? Have I developed myself as a character on the page?

- Have I created a sense of place in my writing? Have I let the physical surroundings seep into my scenes and in and around my dialogue?

- Are there moments when I need to linger in reflection?

- Does my voice serve the purpose of my piece? Does it feel authentic?

- Are there images in my piece that can work on a metaphorical level? Have I drawn these out as much as possible?

Here is an example of how asking these questions can affect your writing as you revise. The following excerpt is from a memoir that one of my former students, Alexis Wolfe, is writing. It's a story about coming to terms with her older son's diagnosis of Charge syndrome, a complex syndrome that occurs in 1 in 9,000–10,000 births. At this point in the story, Alexis and her husband, who are both British, do not have a diagnosis. The story takes place in Surrey, England. It is the same scene written twice, a first-draft version and a revised version. I have also included my comments to Alexis on the first draft to help her see where she could expand the scene when she revised.

From Alexis Wolfe's memoir-in-progress

Version 1:

After the talk with Dr. Haddad we heed Jan's advice, to go for a walk. She promises to make my mum a cup of tea back on the ward and give Jacob his 5 pm feed. Neil and I set off for a walk around the hospital site, finding ourselves in a field behind the mortuary, the chimney tower which I always thought was part of a cremato-rium but actually is an incinerator, casting a long shadow in the late afternoon.

Neil breaks the silence. "This doesn't feel real does it?"

I agree. The whole Jacob thing is surreal and makes no sense. Why us? Then Neil says almost accusingly, "But you knew, didn't you? You must be bloody psychic, you knew something was wrong."

"What?" I was bewildered. "What on earth are you talking about? How could I know this was going to happen?"

"Remember the day you cried at the sink," he said. "You were fine, you were merrily washing up and then out of the blue you couldn't stop crying."

MY COMMENTS TO ALEXIS:

After the talk with Doctor Haddad we heed Jan's advice, to go for a walk. She promises to make my mum a cup of tea back on the ward and give Jacob his 5 pm feed. Neil and I set off for a walk around the hospital site, finding ourselves in a field behind the mortuary, the chimney tower which I always thought was part of a crematorium but actually is an incinerator, casting a long shadow in the late afternoon. *[Use this ominous place. Are you wondering at all if it would have been better if Jacob had died? Even the word "incinerator" brings up so many deadly images in my mind. KH]*

After a while *[How long? What have you been thinking? What sounds do you hear as you walk silently side by side?]* Neil breaks the silence. "This doesn't feel real does it?"

I agree. *[Here I'd love to hear you agree. Do you look at Neil when he asks this? What is surrounding you as you walk? Sounds? Smells? What would have felt "real"?]* The whole Jacob thing is surreal and makes no sense. Why us? Then Neil says almost accusingly, "But you knew, didn't you? You must be bloody psychic, you knew something was wrong." *[What does Neil's face look like as he says this? Does he run his hands through his hair? Purse his lips?]*

"What?" I was bewildered. "What on earth are you talking about? How could I know this was going to happen?" *[Are you angry that he would ask this? I think you can even pause here and wonder whether he has been angry with you. Does he blame you for Jacob's disability? For his birth? Is there a moment when he wishes you had terminated the pregnancy?]*

"Remember the day you cried at the sink" he said. "You were fine, you were merrily washing up and then out of the blue you couldn't stop crying." *[This is really interesting—that he thought you were feeling "merry." That's not exactly how you were feeling that day, and this difference between your real emotions and his perception of your emotions could have some reflection.]*

Version 2:

. . . .

After the talk with Dr. Haddad we decide to heed Jan's advice to go for a walk. There are things that need doing back in Room 8: Jacob's 5 pm feed is looming, his nappy will be bulging. But Jan assures us she can take care of all of this. She even promises to make my mum a cup of tea.

So Neil and I set off for a walk around the hospital site, finding ourselves in a field behind the mortuary, the chimney tower that I always thought was part of a crematorium but is actually an incinerator, is casting a long shadow in the late afternoon. We haven't deliberately headed towards this area, but the need for fresh air and space is overwhelming; we both need to get away from people, from the hustle of the corridors, the relentless comings and goings in the unit and the clatter of the canteen. Here behind the mortuary building is a field—a wide, flat expanse of land. Nothing much to see in the distance, almost a blank canvas, just grass laid out before us, burnt yellow from the summer heat wave, stretching out to the horizon, where it meets with the dusky sky. The grass is overgrown here, above ankle height, making it hard to walk through; we have to lift our feet higher than normal to keep moving. One step at a time, I tell myself, reflecting on Jacob's care and echoing Dr. Haddad's parting words today: let's just take one step at a time. But how do you keep walking when every step takes so much effort? The long grass swishes as we plough on.

After a few minutes we pause side by side. It's clear there is no landmark to head toward; it seems we could stride across this field indefinitely and never arrive anywhere.

Neil breaks the silence. "This doesn't feel real, does it?"

He doesn't look hopeful anymore. He looks crushed. Tired, pale—there are dark circles around his eyes. I know I have these dead eyes too; I noticed them earlier in the mirror in the milk kitchen.

"I know," I say. "It feels like we're trapped in a bad dream. It's like someone detonated a bomb." When Dr. Haddad was talking earlier I was trying to concentrate, but the voice in my head kept saying, *Nah, this can't be real. This isn't happening.* And I couldn't shut it up.

Neil nods. "I just can't stop thinking, *Why us?*" He pauses. "And then I think, well, *Why Not Us?*" He kicks at a small mound of grass and soil.

I see it then, a flicker of frustration in his eyes, and I wonder who he is most angry with: Me? The doctors? Himself? Fate?

"But you knew, didn't you?" he says, almost accusingly. "You must be bloody psychic, 'cause you knew something was wrong."

"What?" I say, bewildered. "What are you talking about? How could I know this was going to happen?" I'm too confused to feel angry at his suggestion; it just seems so utterly absurd.

"Remember the day you cried at the sink?" he said. "You were fine, you were merrily washing up and then out of the blue you couldn't stop crying."

Place does so much more work in the second version of this scene. I love how the grass that Alexis and her husband are trudging through echoes the struggle to take their son's hospitalization and health "one step at a time." I also love how they are walking toward nothing in particular, just as they are plodding ahead with Jacob, not knowing where they will end up.

We also have a much better sense of Alexis's state of mind in lines like this: "When Dr. Haddad was talking earlier I was trying to concentrate, but the voice in my head kept saying, *Nah, this can't be real. This isn't happening.* And I couldn't shut it up."

WRITING EXERCISE: EXPANDING SCENES

Go back to a piece of writing and look at your scenes. Choose one scene and read it as I read Alexis's scene. Make notes. Are there places where you could insert body language? Dialogue rather than summary? Sensory details? Can you allow the surrounding place to more thoroughly seep into the scene? Is there room for lines of thought or backstory? Rewrite your scene, incorporating all of this new writing. How does it feel different?

WRITING EXERCISE: DEVELOPING METAPHOR

Start as you did in the previous exercise: find a piece of writing and read over an important scene. This time, think about metaphor. Are there certain details in the scene or the place where the scene is staged that could work on a metaphorical level (such as the incinerator in Alexis's scene or the long grass through which she and her husband are trudging)? Sometimes we don't realize that a place or detail in a scene can work on a metaphorical level until after we've written it and are able to go back and make those connections. Make a list of details that could work as metaphors in your piece. Free-write on one or more of these things for 10 minutes and then incorporate some of this new writing into the scene. How does this additional writing change your scene?

Another thing to consider as you're revising is how you convey information to the reader. Here is an example from my memoir of how I changed a chapter that contained a lot of free-floating information (in the first draft) to a chapter with the same information imbedded in the scene (the current draft).

In this chapter, Stella develops sepsis, a blood infection, after the IV pulls from the vein in her arm and fills her shoulder with fluid. In the first draft, I had many short paragraphs, alternating between scene and free-floating medical information:

Dr. Brown, who has been Stella's doctor for the last few days, shakes her head. "A setback," she says. "Just yesterday we talked about her being ready to have the IV removed."

She's a petite woman, professional in her blue scrubs, but kind, gentle. She slips her tape recorder, into which all the neonatologists speak as they do their rounds, into her pocket. She puts a hand on my shoulder.

"If we had taken it out yesterday—" She shrugs. "You just never know." She's sympathetic, head tilted to the side. She explains the antibiotics and the blood tests.

I wish I could blame this doctor, hate her for this, but I can't. I wouldn't even have the energy. She smiles before she moves on to Emily, who is still next to Stella, still small, but doing well.

I lean over Stella's isolette and will her to grip my finger, but it's as if I'm not here, not touching her. This would be the time to pray, and I do, sort of, but I don't direct my prayers to anyone in particular; I just send them up, hoping it will make a difference. I press my eyes shut and try to stop the tears and whisper *please let her be okay, please.*

These are the facts: Stella has sepsis, a severe blood infection. She's on two different kinds of antibiotics. Her blood tests won't be back for two days, so they won't know until then which antibiotic she really needs. For now, she will get enough drugs to knock it out, whatever it is. The doctors are being cautious.

A little later in the chapter—after a few paragraphs of scene, I have this, set apart:

> This is what I will learn: anything that breaks the skin barrier—IV lines, ventilators, feeding tubes, blood tests—becomes a path for infection to enter the body. A preemie is too weak to contain a localized infection; it sweeps the tiny body, plunders, invades the blood. Septicemia means: "infection of the blood." Symptoms include pale, mottled skin, chilly hands and feet, irritability, listlessness.
>
> I will read Dr. Manginello's book about preemies and learn that a preemie's veins are brittle, so fragile and narrow that they can break easily. I imagine the veins as frozen strands of wet hair, encased in glistening ice. I imagine them shattering, the IV lines breaking free, filling arms and heads with liquid. This is infiltration. Like war.

I originally sectioned this chapter like this because I thought (hoped) that it would add to the feeling of disorientation I was experiencing that day. But as I was rewriting, I realized it wasn't the most effective way to get the information across, and sectioning it actually decreased the narrative urgency and the reader's understanding of my emotional state in the scene.

Here is basically the same scene in the new draft. (Note that Kally is Stella's nurse. Kris is the nurse from across the room whom I like better.)

> Kally moves away and I just stand there, staring at Stella, not touching her. When I look up again, Dr. Brown is there, spraying foam into her hands. She's a petite woman, professional in her blue

scrubs, but kind, gentle. She nods to Stella. "It's a setback," she says. "Just yesterday we talked about her being ready to have the IV removed, and if we had taken it out yesterday—" She shrugs. "You just never know."

A setback. I resist the urge to get angry. If the IV could have been taken out yesterday, why wasn't it? But Dr. Brown is sympathetic, her head tilted to the side.

"We started her on two different kinds of antibiotics right away. We're not sure which one is the right one, but we'll know that when we get her labs back. Then we'll discontinue the one she doesn't need."

I stare at Stella, at the IV jutting from her skull, and imagine all that medicine being injected into her bloodstream. Some of it will wage war against her infection, some of it will do nothing—a useless bystander on the sidelines of a bloody battle.

I'll learn later that anything that breaks a preemie's skin barrier—IV lines, ventilators, feeding tubes, blood tests—becomes a path for infection to enter the body. I'll learn that a preemie's veins are brittle, fragile, like strands of hair encased in glistening ice. When they crack, an IV line can break free, filling an arm or head with fluid. A preemie is too weak to contain a localized infection, so it sweeps the tiny body, plunders, invades the blood.

Dr. Brown puts her hand on my shoulder. "The antibiotics should take care of this."

I nod, my eyes full of tears. *It should. Should.*

Dr. Brown moves on to Emily, and Kris comes over from the other side of the room and gives me a hug. "Oh sweetie," she says. "I'm so sorry. She was doing so well."

I start to cry harder, enveloped in Kris's floral perfume. Why can't Kris be Stella's nurse? Why can't Kally tell me she's sorry? I pull away and brush the hair from my eyes.

In the first draft I wrote: "She explains the antibiotics and the blood tests." In the second, I let Dr. Brown speak: "We started her on two different kinds of antibiotics right away. We're not sure which one is the right one, but we'll know that when we get her labs back. Then we'll discontinue the one she doesn't need." Instead of a free-floating paragraph, I provide the reader with the information the doctor gave me when she gave it to me. To make the scene less disjointed I also moved some of the other information so that it's in and around this conversation rather than set apart.

WRITING EXERCISE:
IN AND AROUND DIALOGUE

Look back at a piece of writing in which you are trying to get information (backstory or reflection or outside information) across to the reader. Try rewriting the scene using dialogue to reveal the information. Or pull in outside information and insert it in and around your dialogue, as I did above with the information I later learned about preemie veins being brittle. How does bringing this information in and around the dialogue change your scene?

CUTTING IN REVISION

Sometimes revising involves eliminating writing—a lot of writing—and this can be painful. (*What? I wrote 400 pages and now I have to cut 100?*) In Chapter 11, I mentioned that I ended up cutting several chapters from the final version of my memoir. I realized that those chapters weren't needed to convey the story and in fact hindered the telling of the story, so I let them go. Now, I didn't actually delete them from my computer; I pasted them into my "Cut Snippets–Memoir" folder, which grew over the course of the revision to about 70 pages. I don't actually throw anything anyway, because I might turn a cut line or chapter into a different story or essay. You never know when those specific words might come in handy.

Cutting can be liberating, and once you're comfortable with it, it will make your writing stronger. When you're doing final editing before you submit a piece of writing, give yourself a goal: I'm going to cut 10 percent of the words from this piece. It's amazing, but we can almost always tighten our prose. When I was polishing an earlier draft of my memoir, I ended up cutting 25 pages simply by eliminating a sentence here and a sentence there. It's kind of embarrassing, actually. I realized in the process that I had often tacked on an extra, unnecessary sentence at the end of most paragraphs. You always want the last sentence in a paragraph to be the strongest one, and my strongest sentences were often the second-to-last ones. I think this had to do with not trusting the reader, or myself. Hopefully I'm getting better at it, but I'm sure in 20 years I'll look back at some of the writing I'm doing now and wonder why didn't I cut more.

TAKE YOUR TIME

Sometimes, writing feels like trudging through mud. But let it be hard. Give yourself time to muck around in the mud, to explore and write, and explore some more in an effort to discover the true story in your writing. No one ever said this was easy. And if someone *did* say it was easy, they were lying.

Also, take time away from a piece of writing when you can. Whether it's a week or a year, time away from your words can help you see them with new eyes. Don't rush into the revision process. Let the last draft simmer in your consciousness before diving back into it. I think a good indication of whether you are ready to revise is whether you understand the true story you're telling. But sometimes it's just a gut feeling: you feel ready to go back to it. I have several short stories from graduate school that have been languishing on my computer and in a folder for six years now. I know that a couple of them have potential, but I haven't been ready to dive back into them and rewrite them. I'm ready now, and I'm really looking forward to it.

The inspiration for a piece might have been written years ago. Maybe you tried to write it but couldn't, because you needed emotional distance from the material, or maybe you couldn't figure out how to approach or revise the topic yet. Regardless, never throw that writing away. Save it on your computer or in a file. When you're ready to write and revise, those pieces will be there.

Susan Ito's "Samuel" (from Chapter 8) originally began as a poem. Ito says, "I wrote the original poem from which 'Samuel' grew about a week after we lost him. I put it away until many years later, when I expanded it into an essay, which after *many* revisions became 'Samuel,' in the anthology *It's a Boy*. All in all, I think it's gone through about 20 revisions over 19 years."

This is Ito's original poem:

Bee Sting

· ·

"It's just going to be a bee sting," the doctor said
And it was,
a small tingle
quick pricking bubbles
under my navel
and then a thing like a tiny
drinking straw
that went
in and out
with a barely audible pop
fast
so fast I almost didn't have time to whisper
"I love you"
and then
a bandaid unwrapped
with its plastic smell of childhood
and spread onto my belly
"All done," he said.
All done.

My child was inside
swallowing the fizzy drink
and it bubbled against his tiny tongue
like a bud
the deadly soda pop
(this little boy won't be sitting on the front steps
in his gym shorts
drinking Coke out of a green glass bottle)
while I lay on my side pinching the pillowcase
and wondered,
is he afraid?

> can he feel my sorrow
> flooding around him?
> His father sat on a chair
> next to the bed
> and held my hand lightly
> and I looked over his shoulder
> into the dark slice of window
> between the heavy curtains
> and the child
> jumped against my hand
> leaping through
> the darkness
> and then
> was gone
> all gone.

Many of the lines from this original version did make it into "Samuel." So hang on to those early drafts, even if you aren't ready to revise them yet.

One last thing I want to say about the revision process is that it always helps to have trusted people read your work. We are so close to our own writing that sometimes it's difficult for us to see it in a new way. Readers can help you identify the true story and where the possibilities of your piece lie. They can also help you cut unnecessary sections and point out where you need to expand. I know my writing group has made a world of difference in my writing. It is so much stronger for their thoughtful critiques.

But how do you find trusted readers? If you have a literary center in your town, that's a great place to start. Many of the students in my classes continue meeting after class is over. You can also connect with mother writers through blogs or social media and start an in-person or virtual writing group. The important thing is to choose people who are writers or are interested in writing. Your spouse may or may not be the best choice. I let Donny read my writing, but from him I want cheerleading, not a critique (though I'll accept that, too, if he offers it). So be clear on what kind of feedback you want and how you like to receive the feedback.

But don't forget to give yourself the time you need to muck around in your writing and make it as strong as possible. Don't rush revision.

CHAPTER 13

PUBLISHING:
FROM BLOGS TO BOOKS

MY FIRST ACCEPTED ESSAY WAS A PIECE I WROTE
for a local parenting magazine. I had e-mailed it to the editor in mid-October, and as Christmas neared and I still hadn't heard from her I assumed she wasn't interested. But then one evening, as I sat in front of our old, very slow computer in the basement, I saw an e-mail from this editor pop into my inbox. I almost didn't open it because I didn't want to read a rejection letter just before bed. But I decided I better get it over with, and when I opened it and read that she was interested in the essay—she wanted it!—I let out a squeal so loud (and apparently animal-like) that Donny thought I had injured myself. When he tromped down the stairs, expecting to find me twisted in pain, I shouted, "Finally!" and promptly burst into tears. After years of hard work and dozens of rejection letters, I felt, for the first time, justified. I walked around in a happy daze for a week, thinking, I *am* a writer. I really am.

Sending your writing out into the world is a wonderful step to take, but before you do so, it's important to think about the ramifications of writing other people's lives.

WRITING ABOUT YOUR CHILDREN

The goal of this book is to help you write your motherhood stories, to capture and examine the varied experiences we have as mothers. Some of you may never want to publish what you've written, but some of you will. In Chapter 10, I quoted Annie Dillard, who said that you don't want to kick around "people who don't have access to a printing press." This is true when we write about anyone, but it's especially true when we are writing about our children, who have no control over what we say about them. They might not actually care that we write about them. They might actually like being "famous." Regardless, they also depend on us to protect them.

I try not to write anything about my children that might make them feel that I've betrayed them. Now, that's not to say that they might not be hurt by some of the things I say about motherhood, but I hope that before they're interested in reading that material, I can sit down and talk to them about what motivated me to write and publish it.

The topic of privacy and writing our children's lives always comes up in my classes. One of my students posed the following questions: "What if they don't appreciate my efforts to examine my motherhood later in life? Even more scary, what if they are angry that I wrote about their naked escapades in the yard, or extended nursing?" Another student said, "It feels great to write [essays about my children], but there's part of me that feels relief that none of the ones I've submitted have been published."

Others don't worry about writing about their children. One student said that she didn't think her son would be angry with her for writing their lives as long as she "owned her truth." She added, "We are often so isolated in this world, at loss for community, and it is through sharing our stories that we can create connections. What a wonderful gift to have someone write truth and be able to allow the reader to connect to that truth."

I really agree with this. To me, owning one's truth has to do with the ability to really interrogate yourself, as I mentioned in Chapter 10. If you are self-serving, memoir doesn't work.

I also think that talking openly about your writing and why it's important to you helps your children (and everyone else) understand how critical it is for you to be able to express yourself through words.

I am more careful when I write about my children on my blog than I am when I write about them in print publications. I write about them infrequently on my blog partly because the blog isn't really about my kids; it's about reading and writing and teaching and the push-and-pull of trying to balance a writing life and motherhood. Partly, I'm more careful writing about my kids on my blog because of the confessional nature of blogging.

Emily Bazelon, in her article "Is This Tantrum on the Record?: The ground rules for writing about your kids," published in *Slate* magazine, challenged writers (and particularly bloggers) to consider whether there are, or should be, ground rules when you write about your children. She said, "When I write about my kids, I'm not only thinking as their mother. I'm also thinking as a professional writer. Those two identities don't always align—they just don't. I like to think that when there's tension, I err on the side of protecting my kids' interests, steering clear of any material that's too embarrassing or private."

In this article Bazelon quoted author Steve Almond, who, with his wife, co-wrote the blog *BabyDaddy* on Babble.com. But when their daughter, Josie, was 18 months old, they retired the blog because, as Almond said, "The blog medium has a certain kind of immediacy, and a reciprocal surrendering of privacy, that we don't want in our lives forever—and that Josie may not want, either."

It's the immediacy and accessibility of blogs that make me cautious. I post the occasional anecdote about Stella or Zoë, recounting something funny or adorable that they said. But in the back of my mind, there is always a flashing red light reminding me of the potential Googling power of a gaggle of 12-year-olds. At some point, my daughters may want to read what I've written about them, and I don't want them to feel exposed or betrayed if and when they do.

I'm always curious how other mother writers balance their children's privacy with their need to write, so when I have the opportunity to ask about this, I do. I love what novelist and essayist Julie Schumacher says:

> There's an ethical dilemma in being a parent and a writer of realistic fiction (or nonfiction), that is, a person whose real life and relationships can be a starting point for creative work. When your children are very young, you're free to comment on their behavior—as well as your own parenting skills—in their presence; as they get older, they don't want to be the subjects even of positive conversation ("Look how she's grown!"). That said, I think writers can model responsible self-inquiry—Who am I? What does my life mean?—and demonstrate to their children that creating art, and asking difficult and sometimes unanswerable questions about relationships, families, and societies, is part of living an examined life.
>
> When I have published nonfiction about my children, I've gotten permission from them first. Fiction offers a bit more of a cover; still, I've asked my children to read each of my young adult novels—including *Black Box*—before they were published. I think my kids understand what are for me the two enormous truths of this parenting/writing experience: 1) I love my children wildly, unreservedly, and 2) I can't live my life without writing things down.

Beth Kephart, of "The Line Is White and It Is Narrow" and *A Slant of Sun*, said:

> I want to say first and absolutely that it is very difficult terrain, writing the truth, and that while I am moved deeply to write

about those things and people I love, I have taught myself, over time, to keep most of that love within, and to put my passion toward fiction, fable, poetry, and history. I wrote a trilogy of memoir—one about loving a child, one about friends, one about marriage. I made a very conscious decision not to write about my son after sixth grade. I wanted him to be completely free from any historic language from then on. I make vague references to him from time to time on my blog, but only because he is a person of such great importance in my life, and not because I feel I am free to report on his own stories.

There is no right or wrong way to write about motherhood and your children, but I do recommend thinking about these ethical issues when you are ready to publish your writing, whether it's on a blog, in a literary journal, or in a book.

HOW TO "GET OUT THERE"

There are a number of approaches you can take if you're interested in sending your writing out into the world.

BLOGGING

Blogging can be a powerful tool for writers. It's a wonderful way to develop your writer's voice and get you in the habit of writing regularly. It's also an effective way to build your platform and develop a readership for your writing.

I started my blog in early 2007 for three reasons: to extend the reach of my classes; to develop interest in my memoir; and to create a place online where motherhood literature would be taken seriously as art. I blog about teaching, writing, and motherhood, about how and where these things intersect, and I also review motherhood literature and interview authors on my blog.

What I didn't expect when I began blogging is that I would become part of such a rich and varied community of women who are doing the same thing I'm doing: living and mothering and trying to get words on the page. Through my blog, I've met hundreds of other mother writers and developed friendships with women around the world.

Motherhood can be isolating. My mom recently noted how much more challenging it is for my sister and me to connect with other mothers than it was for her when she was a new mother. I think she's right. Most of my friends with children work, at least part-time, and we all have different schedules. Playdates are squeezed in between work and teaching, between grocery shopping and dance class. And even the emphasis is different: playdates are for the kids, a chance for them to play with each other. Ideally, it's also an opportunity for parents to talk with one another, but in many cases, that goal is secondary.

But the Internet and blogging have provided a different way for mothers to connect with one another and become part of a large, diverse community. Mothers are laying claim to a virtual room of their own, one that can be accessed from just about anywhere on the map.

This sense of community cannot be overestimated. One of my lovely students recently wrote this on her blog:

> I began blogging as an exercise in discipline. I needed to commit to writing on a regular basis, and I switched from my Word document to a blogging interface in part because WordPress is a prettier notepad on which to write. Perhaps there was also a part of me that wanted the affirmation of an audience or a community, and I didn't want to be at the mercy of a faceless editor to get that affirmation.
>
> As a novice blogger I really had no idea how to get this audience, and I was content with having my childhood friend as my sole reader. But the more I blogged and the more blogs I

read, unexpected things happened: readers came over, and they left comments or e-mailed me. They liked what I wrote and responded with encouragement. Some even returned for more and passed my link on to their friends. I realized, then, that I was no longer writing to a faceless audience. I felt an incredible surge in energy when I received this kind of feedback. My motivation to write increased, and I felt lifted by this new community of like-minded mother writers. In a short span of time, I had built a very small but warm community of readers and—dare I say— friends. I began to gain more confidence and even pride in my words and my ideas, and this spurred me to keep writing.

Blogging is the thing that keeps some writers writing regularly, and in the process of posting weekly and reading other people's blogs a sense of community emerges. There is a tremendous amount of power in that.

If you are interested in blogging, there are a few things to consider before you write your first post:

Purpose

What will be the purpose of your blog? Is it to share stories about your children with extended family and friends? To work through some of the frustrations or transformations inherent in parenting? To help develop your writing voice and be accountable to your writing goals? Is your goal to develop a readership for your work, to test out essay ideas before you polish them and submit them? It's your blog, and it can be whatever you want it to be, but it's helpful to have an idea of what "it" is. This will help you stay focused and find a niche in the very crowded blogosphere.

Privacy

Before you start blogging, it's also important to decide how much personal information about yourself and your family you'll share on your blog. Will you use your real name and the names of your family members? Will you post photos? Some people use pseudonyms or initials. Some people limit who can read certain posts (or their entire blogs) by making them accessible only with a password. Having a sense of your blog's purpose will help you decide how public you want to be on your blog.

For instance, I use my full name on my blog because my blog is partly a marketing tool. I'm trying to develop a readership for my books and interest in my classes, workshops, and retreats. I use Stella and Zoë's real names because I use their real names in my non-blog writing, much of which is available online. But I don't use their last name, which is different from my own, and I never post photos of them or reveal such details as where they go to school or take swimming lessons. I also don't use my husband's name on my blog—I just refer to him as "D." This is because when I started the blog he was teaching in the public schools, and, as unlikely as it might be, I didn't want anything I wrote to affect his position. I wanted to protect his privacy, and I didn't want to get his approval for every post I wrote. Of course, anyone who has read this book or my memoir knows his name is Donny, but I still prefer to keep it off my blog.

Blogging is a wonderful way to connect with other writers and mothers and can also be a sounding board for developing your own writing.

SUBMITTING TO JOURNALS

Submitting essays to journals and magazines is a great way to begin to make a name for yourself as a writer. I hope you'll do this at some point, but I also want to encourage you not to feel rushed to publish. After you have moved past the discovery draft of a piece of writing and have begun to re-vision it as discussed in Chapter 12, take time away from your writing if possible. Continue to ask, *What is this really about?* Having an answer to this question will help you know when your writing is ready to be submitted.

When you *do* feel a piece of writing is ready to go out into the world, ask a few trusted readers to offer feedback. As I mention in Chapter 12, pick people who are writers or avid readers to read your work. You can have them read for coherence and for typing errors. We are so close to our own stories that it's easy to miss errors or not realize which passages need to be further developed, so it's always helpful to have another set of eyes take a look at your piece before you submit it.

Then, do your research. Familiarize yourself with what types of pieces literary journals and magazines are publishing. (See "Suggested Reading" in the Appendix for a few journals where you can submit your writing.) Find a journal that seems like the best fit and send it there. Don't blindly send your writing to 25 different publications. You are wasting time and postage.

You can also try pitching your writing to non-motherhood journals or glossy magazines. A great resource for pitching to glossy magazines (and for agent and book queries as well) is novelist and freelance writer Allison Winn Scotch's blog, *Ask Allison*. Over the years she has answered tons of questions about querying editors and pitching articles, so search her archives before you e-mail her.

Most motherhood journals accept writing from previously unpublished writers, though it does help to have clips (published pieces) when you submit your writing. As one of my students pointed out, this feels like a Catch-22: How can I get a clip if no one will publish my writing? One way to approach this is to submit first to small, local magazines or journals and then work your way up to larger publications.

But even if you have found a journal that you think is a fit for a piece of writing, don't be discouraged if you are rejected. It's wonderful to get writing accepted by a journal, magazine, editor, or agent, but know that most published writers have a tall stack of rejection letters sitting next to their acceptances.

REJECTION

I don't know any writer who likes receiving rejection letters, but rejections are part of being a writer. To have your writing accepted, it will also have to be rejected. There have been periods in my writing life when my day didn't feel complete unless I received at least one rejection letter. Those periods felt endless.

A few years ago, after one particularly nasty rejection by an agent, I burst into tears. I sobbed for a full 10 minutes. Then Donny and Stella, who was three years old at the time, hugged me tightly and told me they loved me and that the agent was crazy. When I calmed down a bit (though I was still blotchy and red-faced), I laced up my running shoes, cranked the volume on my iPod, and ran the fastest seven miles I'd ever run, alternating between laughter, tears, and cursing. (I'm sure passersby thought I was completely insane.) Later that night, I drank a couple of glasses of wine and thought mean thoughts about the agent. A few days later, I was ready to send out more query letters.

Rejection gets easier, and sometimes an encouraging and complimentary rejection is almost as good—almost—as an acceptance. But whether a rejection is encouraging or not, I always save it. I tuck it in a folder in the file cabinet in my basement or move it to the rejection folder in my e-mail inbox. Sometimes I go for a run. Sometimes I pour myself a glass of wine. And the following day, I sit back down at my desk and do the work of a writer: I write and revise and submit my writing.

Rejection is a necessary evil, but on some level I think it forces you to believe more strongly in your work. One of my students recently asked how you know whether you should keep sending out a piece of writing or wake up and smell the coffee and just call it quits. I don't think you should ever call it quits. Maybe you need to put your writing aside for a while and look at it again in a few months. It's true that sometimes a rejection means a piece is not ready: Maybe it needs a little tweaking. Maybe it needs serious revision. But maybe it *is* ready and you simply haven't found the right editor or the right magazine. I know writers who will send out a story or essay 15 times before they revise. If you believe in what you're doing and believe there is a market for it, don't give up!

I love the stories about award-winning writers who were rejected a gazillion times before their books were acquired. Kate DiCamillo's first children's novel, *Because of Winn-Dixie*, which won a Newbery Honor award and was made into a movie, was rejected over 100 times before it was finally acquired. And if you count the rejections DiCamillo received before *Winn-Dixie*, the total number of rejections she received before her big acceptance was over 400! That's a lot of rejection letters, but she didn't give up. DiCamillo says, "I decided a long time ago that I didn't have to be talented. I just had to be persistent [...]."

PITCHING BOOKS

There are a couple of ways to approach pitching a book. If you think your story has commercial appeal—that it would sell to a wide audience—you may want to try to get an agent. You need an agent to approach the larger publishing houses and you may want one to approach smaller houses as well. Agents cultivate relationships with editors throughout the industry, and they use those relationships to get editors to pay attention to your book. They also negotiate contracts on your behalf and can sell the subsidiary rights to your book in order to bring your story out in as many forms (ebook, audio book, TV, movie) and as many markets (including foreign markets) as possible. But keep in mind that you can approach many of the smaller publishing houses on your own, without an agent.

FINDING AN AGENT OR EDITOR

Sometimes being published in a journal can help you attract the attention of an agent. Sometimes, agents approach popular bloggers to write a book. But don't count on these methods alone. Finding the right agent is important, and most likely you'll need to query agents to attract their interest. One way to start building a list of agents that might be a fit for your manuscript is to go to the bookstore and flip through the acknowledgment pages of books that are comparable to yours. Authors almost always thank their agents in the acknowledgments, so this is a great place to start. Another way is to consult industry guides that list agents, editors, and publishing houses.

Searching the shelf at the bookstore is also a great way to find small presses that might be a fit for your book. Which small presses publish parenting memoirs or literary memoirs? Do as much research as you can at this stage, because narrowing the list of appropriate publishers will help you decide whom to send your manuscript to first.

Once you have your list to query, send your letters and submissions out to multiple agents or small presses simultaneously and according to their submission guidelines, which are usually stated on their websites. If the agent or editor is not interested, you may receive a rejection letter or you may not receive a response at all. If an agent or editor is interested in your work, he or she may ask to see your proposal or full manuscript. Be personable and professional in all of your communications. Agents and editors want to know about you and your book, and they also want to see if you are someone with whom they could work closely.

It's important to remember that agents and editors are people, and these relationships are important. Just because an agent is interested in representing you or an editor wants to acquire your book doesn't mean you have to sign with her. You want your agent and editor to "get" you, to be excited about and see the potential in what you're doing. You want to work with someone who believes in you.

If you do find an agent or editor who is interested in your book, don't be surprised if she wants you to revise or rethink sections of your manuscript. This kind of collaboration can be invaluable and really strengthen your book or proposal. But if an agent or editor wants you to turn your book into something you don't want it to be, that's a sign that you should be working with someone else.

A great way to meet agents and editors is at writing conferences. Writing conferences often offer workshops on craft and publishing, and also opportunities to meet face-to-face with agents and editors. These kinds of connections are important. If you've met an agent or editor in person, he or she will generally give your submission more attention than a blind submission through e-mail or snail mail. I know a number of writers who ended up signing with an agent they met at a conference.

Always make sure your work is the best you can make it before you contact an agent or editor. I remember thinking, erroneously, that once I had an agent, my memoir would sell—that "getting an agent" equaled "book sale." I also assumed that my first agent would help me make my memoir better than it was. I thought she would have revision suggestions and that we'd work together on my manuscript. (Clearly, I had an inkling that it wasn't yet the best book I could write.) But my agent didn't offer suggestions—she sent it out into the world and it was rejected on a first round of submissions to publishers.

I learned two important lessons through this process: I needed to be absolutely confident in my work before it was sent to editors, and, for my next project, I wanted an editorial agent, someone who would be willing to roll up her sleeves and jump into the mud of my manuscript with me. I found my current agent by querying another agent who had represented a mothering book. He didn't think this book would be a good fit for his list, but he recommended I contact a colleague. I did, and when she expressed interest in representing me, we spoke on the phone. One of the questions I asked her was whether she considered herself an editorial agent. She did—and is!—and I'm so grateful for her insights.

When you are pitching your book to agents and editors, remember that rejection does not necessarily mean your book isn't good. Rejections often have to do with money or the fact that a book doesn't fit with a publisher's list. Agents will always ask themselves whether they can make money from your book: if they can't sell your book, they don't make money. An editor will look at what their house is already publishing, how those books sold, and whether your book will be able to stand out on their list.

PATIENCE

Patience and persistence are necessary in all stages of the writing process, but they come in particularly handy if you are working on a book-length manuscript. You not only need patience to write and revise and rethink and rework your writing; you need patience and persistence as you begin to pitch your book to agents or editors.

I am not a naturally patient person, but as a writer I have had to learn to be patient. So much of a writer's time—at least *this* writer's time—is spent waiting, thinking, revising, waiting. Did I mention waiting? I wait for letters to come back from journals. I wait for responses from editors. I wait for calls from my agent. I wait and I wait and I wait. And as I wait, I sometimes become discouraged. I keep working on new writing—or rewriting—and I keep teaching and thinking about craft. But still, there are times I have wondered if the waiting would ever pay off.

A couple of years ago, when I was feeling particularly discouraged with my writing—nothing was happening, no one was buying my memoir—one of the orchids that line our dining room windows bloomed. Most of these orchids were given to us by Mimi, with whom Donny and I lived just after we were married. As I described in the excerpt from my memoir in Chapter 9, Mimi always gave me credit when her orchids bloomed, and I always smiled at her insistence, even when I knew I couldn't take credit for her orchids' glory.

Mimi died when Stella was two, a couple of years after Donny and I had moved to our own house. When we went back to Mimi's house for the memorial service, I stared at the greenhouse where I had spent so many hours and which was so very important to Mimi, and I began to cry. I couldn't imagine those flowers gone, her collection sold or given away. Finally, between sobs, I asked her daughter-in-law if it would be OK if I chose one of the orchids. She kindly agreed, and I chose one of Mimi's favorites: the hanging Vanda Rothschildiana. Its flower, when it blooms, is three different shades of lavender and as big as a child's hand.

I cared for the Vanda in our house for three years. I watered it, repotted it, covered its roots in new wood chips and fertilizer. But it never bloomed for me—I assumed that our house wasn't humid enough. Then, one spring day, when I took it to the sink to spray it down, I saw, peeking from beneath its narrow leaves, a long, thin bud. I gasped. The Vanda, finally. I called Donny at work and squealed the news into the phone. "We just have to be patient," I said. "It's a reminder that things will happen when they're supposed to."

If Mimi could have seen the Vanda when it bloomed two weeks later, she would have given me a hug and told me I was a genius. My first instinct would have been to shake my head and tell her I had done nothing. But that wouldn't be true. I groomed and watered this plant, cared for it in her absence. And I waited. I was patient. And I knew that this—patience—is the thing she had been congratulating me for all those years ago.

Patience is more important than I ever realized, especially for a writer. Every time you feel like giving up, tucking your manuscript or stack of essays in a drawer, take a deep breath, remind yourself why you are writing, and sit back down at your desk. If you keep working on your craft, keep practicing and re-visioning your writing, publication will come. Don't give up.

CHAPTER 14

KEEPING THE MOMENTUM GOING

IT'S CHALLENGING TO FIND TIME TO WRITE WHEN you are busy with family and a household and work and the general messiness of life. But I hope that as you've worked your way through this book, you've also realized how important it is to set aside time for writing and reading. I hope you've realized how powerful it can be, as Kathleen Hirsch and Katrina Kenison said, to "give voice to the powerful emotions and fears that swirl deep beneath the surface of our daily lives, informing and shaping our relationships with our children and the world at large."

One of the things I suggested in the Introduction is to figure out when and how writing can fit into your life. I hope, as you read this book and tried the writing exercises, you have identified how often and what times of day work best for you to write. But I know it can still be challenging to take that time and make writing a priority in your life.

After Zoë was born, Donny took a new job that required him to travel a lot. (When Zoë was five weeks old, he was actually gone for 11 days. It wasn't pretty, people. I finally told him not to call me at night before bed because by that point I was so exhausted—and furious with him—that the last thing I wanted to do was hear his voice.) I struggled through Zoë's first summer, trying to juggle my daughters' needs with my own. I tried to run and walk when I had a chance, but that wasn't enough for me. I needed to write again. When Donny's schedule eased up a bit at the end of the summer, we worked out a schedule so I could get back to my writing. I got up early and went to the coffee shop from 7:00 to 9:00 a.m. each day. He went into work a little late, and stayed later. After just a week of this schedule, I felt like myself again—I was happier and more patient, and I could truly enjoy the hours I had with my children.

I think it's hard for women—especially mothers—to carve out the time we need for ourselves, whether it's time to go for a run, meet a friend at the coffee shop, or write.

The following piece by Judith Ortiz Cofer gives us, as mothers who are juggling 12 different things, permission to do just that. It gives us a nudge in the right direction, reminds us that we cannot wait for the time to write; we have to *make* time to write.

Five A.M.: Writing as Ritual

An act of will that changed my life from that of a frustrated artist, waiting to have a room of my own and an independent income before getting down to business, to that of a working writer: I decided to get up two hours before my usual time, to set my alarm for 5:00 a.m.

When people ask me how I started writing, I find myself describing the urgent need that I felt to work with language as a search; I did not know for a long time what I was looking for. Although I married at nineteen, had a child at twenty-one—all the while going through college and graduate school *and* working part-time—it was not enough. There was something missing in my life that I came close to only when I turned to my writing, when I took a break from my thesis research to write a poem or an idea for a story on the flip side of an index card. It wasn't until I traced this feeling to its source that I discovered both the cause and the answer to my frustration: I needed to write. I showed my first efforts to a woman, a "literary" colleague, who encouraged me to mail them out. One poem was accepted for publication, and I was hooked. This bit of success is really the point where my problem began.

Once I finished graduate school, I had no reason to stay at the library that extra hour to write poems. It was 1978. My daughter was five years old and in school during the day while I traveled the county, teaching freshman composition on three different campuses. Afternoons I spent taking her to her ballet, tap, and every other socializing lesson her little heart desired. I composed my lectures on Florida's I-95, and that was all the thinking time I had. Does this sound like the typical superwoman's lament? To me it meant being in a constant state of mild anxiety that I could not really discuss with others. What was I to say to them? I need an hour to start a poem? Will someone please stop the world from spinning so fast?

I did not have the privilege of attending a writer's workshop as a beginning writer. I came to writing instinctively, as a dowser finds an underground well. I did not know that I would eventually make a career out of writing books and giving readings of my work. The only models I knew were the unattainable ones: the first famous poet I met was Richard Eberhart, so exalted and venerable that he might as well have been the pope. All I knew at that time was that at twenty-six years of age I felt spiritually deprived, although I had all the things my women friends found sufficiently fulfilling in a "woman's life," plus more; I was also teaching, which is the only vocation I always knew I had. But I had found poetry, or it had found me, and it was demanding its place in my life.

After trying to stay up late at night for a couple of weeks and discovering that there was not enough of me left after a full day of giving to others, I relented and did this odious thing: I set my alarm for 5:00. The first day I shut if off because I could: I had placed it within arm's reach. The second day I set two clocks, one on my night table, as usual, and one out in the hallway. I had to jump out of bed and run to silence it before my family was awakened and the effort nullified. This is when my morning writing ritual that I follow to this day began. I get up at five and put on a pot of coffee. Then I sit in my rocking chair and read what I did the previous day until the coffee is ready. I take fifteen minutes to drink two cups of coffee while my computer warms up—not that it needs to—I just like to see it glowing in the room where I sit in semidarkness, its screen prompting "ready": ready whenever you are. When I'm ready, I write.

Since that first morning in 1978 when I rose in the dark to find myself in a room of my own—with two hours belonging only to me ahead of me, two prime hours when my mind was still filtering my dreams—I have not made or accepted too many excuses for not writing. This apparently ordinary choice, to get up early and to work every day, forced me to come to terms with the discipline of the art. I wrote my poems in this manner for nearly ten years before my first book was published. When I decided to give my storytelling impulse full rein and write a novel, I divided my two hours: the first hour for poetry, the second for fiction; two pages minimum per day. Well or badly, I wrote two pages a day for three and one-half years. This is how my novel, *The Line of the Sun*, was finished. If I had waited to have the time, I would still be waiting to write my novel.

My life has changed considerably since those early days when I was trying to be everything to everyone. My daughter is now twenty-five and in graduate school, not a ballerina, Rockette, or horsewoman but a disciplined student and a self-assured young person. Thus I do not regret the endless hours of sitting in tiny chairs at the Rock-Ette Academy of Dance or of breathing the saturated air at the stables as I waited for her. She got out of her activities something like what I got out of getting up in the dark to work: the feeling that you are in control, in the saddle, on your toes. Empowerment is what the emerging artist needs to win for herself. And the initial sense of urgency to create can easily be dissipated because it entails making the one choice many people, especially women, in our society with its emphasis on the "acceptable" priorities, feel selfish about making: taking the time to create, stealing it from yourself if that's the only way.

Taking the time to create, stealing it from yourself if that's the only way. I love these lines, and I hope you'll learn to do this if you haven't already.

I am a morning writer, but I can't write every day, especially when I'm teaching three classes. I now have three mornings a week to go to the coffee shop to work. I wish I could also write after the kids are in bed, but like Ortiz Cofer, by the end of the day I'm spent and I don't have the creative energy I need to write. I don't write every day; I don't even get to my creative writing (either new material or revising older material) each week. And I'm OK with that. I know I'll get back to it. It helps to have a month here or there to focus on my writing. During those months I still need to tend to other things—the blog, reading and reviewing books, freelance editing, proposals for conferences—but I try to write at least one hour before I move on to my other work. It's slow, slower than I ever would have imagined, but I just keep plugging along.

How does writing fit into *your* life? Take a few minutes to think about what's realistic and jot down a possible writing schedule. This is the first step in making writing a priority in your life. But you also need the support of your family. In a piece I wrote for the anthology *Women Writing on Family*, I discussed this very thing, stressing the importance of communication with your family members in helping you stick to your writing schedule: "If you have a partner, talk to him or her about what writing means in your life and work out a schedule. If you are home with kids during the day, maybe Saturday mornings become your writing time. Or maybe your partner takes the kids to the park and gets them ready for bed one evening a week, so you can head to the library to write."

Juggling writing and motherhood can be challenging, but it's important work, work that can change lives, break down barriers, and dissolve taboos. It's work that creates community—a community that can stretch farther and wider than we ever imagined. So don't give up; keep writing.

CLUSTERING

Clustering is a technique developed by Gabriel Rico (from her book *Writing the Natural Way*). It's a stream-of-consciousness exercise that can help provide an opening into writing and help you move out of feeling stuck. How it works: Write a word denoting a place or a person or a memory in the middle of your page and circle it. Now write the first associations that come to mind and circle those as well, connecting the bubbles with lines. Don't censor or edit yourself. Let whatever comes out come out. Once you have exhausted one train of thought, go back to the original word and see if you are led in a new direction.

Here is an example. I begin with "NICU" (neonatal intensive care unit), where Stella spent a month after she was born. This is based on my first visit to the unit after Stella's birth. (Excuse the handwriting: I was trying to be neat, but it looks like chicken scratch.)

READING QUESTIONS

Writing and reading go hand in hand. As you read the pieces in the book, pay close attention to how they are crafted. Try to identify what works or doesn't work for you. Don't feel that you have to like all the pieces. When we don't like something, identifying the "why" helps us with our own writing. The following questions might be helpful as you think about how certain pieces are put together.

Concrete Details
How does the author use concrete details to ground her writing? Can you point to specific details that invite you into the piece and make it feel real?

Character
How do you know the characters in the piece? Can you describe them? Point to specific lines and scenes that give you a sense of who the characters really are.

Voice
Who is speaking in the piece? How do you know this author? Describe her voice, who she is. Are there specific phrases or lines that she uses to help create this persona? Can you identify the different voices (innocent and experienced) in the piece? Are there other voices at work as well?

Reflection
Is the narrator a reflective narrator? Is she thinking and trying to make sense of her lived experiences on the page? How does she enter into reflection? Is it "placed," grounded in scene, or free-floating?

Structure
How is the piece of writing constructed? Does it tell a chronological story? How does the author incorporate backstory? Can you describe the stage or frame of the piece?

How can it be a model?
What writing strategies employed by the author can you use in your own writing? Are there things you admire about her writing that you would like to try yourself? What experiments can you try in your own writing based on this piece?

SUGGESTED READING

This is not an exhaustive list, just a place to start.

On Craft and the Writing Life

Ellis, Sherry, ed. *Now Write! Nonfiction.*

Garrigues, Lisa. *Writing Motherhood: Tapping Into Your Creativity as a Mother and a Writer.*

Goldberg, Natalie. *Writing Down the Bones: Freeing the Writer Within.*

Gornick, Vivian. *The Situation and the Story: The Art of Personal Narrative.*

Hampl, Patricia. *I Could Tell You Stories: Sojourns in the Land of Memory.*

Kallet, Marilyn, and Judith Ortiz Cofer, eds. *Sleeping With One Eye Open: Women Writers and the Art of Survival.*

Lamott, Anne. *Bird by Bird: Some Instructions on Writing and Life.*

Miller, Brenda, and Suzanne Paola. *Tell It Slant: Writing and Shaping Creative Nonfiction.*

Root, Robert L., and Michael Steinberg. *The Fourth Genre: Contemporary Writers of/on Creative Nonfiction.*

Silverman, Sue William. *Fearless Confessions: A Writer's Guide to Memoir.*

Zinsser, William. *On Writing Well: The Classic Guide to Writing Nonfiction.*

Motherhood Memoirs and Essays

Anderson, Kyra, and Vicki Forman. *Gravity Pulls You In: Perspectives on Parenting Children on the Autism Spectrum.*

Belkin, Lisa. *Life's Work: Confessions of an Unbalanced Mom.*

Berry, Cecelie S., ed. *Rise Up Singing: Black Women Writers on Motherhood.*

Buchanan, Andrea. *Mother Shock: Loving Every (Other) Minute of It.*

———, ed., *It's a Girl* and *It's a Boy.*

———, and Amy Hudock, eds. *Literary Mama: Reading for the Maternally Inclined.*

Cervin, Tina, and Susan Ito. *A Ghost at Heart's Edge: Stories and Poems of Adoption.*

Conlon, Faith, and Gail Hudson. *I Wanna Be Sedated: 30 Writers on Parenting Teenagers.*

Edelman, Hope. *The Possibility of Everything.*

Erdrich, Louise. *The Blue Jay's Dance: A Birth Year.*

Evans, Elrena, and Caroline Grant, eds. *Mama, PhD: Women Write about Motherhood and Academic Life.*

Finger, Anne. *Past Due: A Story of Disability, Pregnancy and Birth.*

Fennelly, Beth Ann. *Great with Child: Letters to a Young Mother.*

Forman, Vicki. *This Lovely Life: A Memoir of Premature Motherhood.*

Groneberg, Jennifer Graf. *Road Map to Holland: How I Found My Way Through My Son's First two Years with Down Syndrome.*

Gwartney, Debra. *Live Through This: A Mother's Memoir of Runaway Daughters and Reclaimed Love.*

Hall, Meredith. *Without a Map.*

Harper, Lisa Catherine. *A Double Life: Discovering Motherhood.*

Harrison, Kathy. *One Small Boat: The Story of a Little Girl Lost Then Found.*

Huber, Sonya. *Cover Me: A Health Insurance Memoir.*

Kamata, Suzanne, ed. *Love You to Pieces: Creative Writers on Raising a Child with Special Needs.*

———. *Call Me Okaasan: Adventures in Multicultural Mothering.*

Kenison, Katrina. *The Gift of an Ordinary Day: A Mother's Memoir.*

Kephart, Beth. *A Slant of Sun: One Child's Courage.*

————. *Still Love in Strange Places: A Memoir.*

Kruger, Pamela, and Jill Smolowe. *A Love Like No Other: Stories from Adoptive Parents.*

Lamott, Anne. *Operating Instructions: A Journal of My Son's First Year.*

Margulis, Jennifer. *Toddler: Real-Life Stories of Those Fickle, Irrational, Urgent, Tiny People We Love.*

McCracken, Elizabeth. *An Exact Replica of a Figment of My Imagination.*

Moses, Kate, and Camille Peri, eds. *Mothers Who Think: Tales of Real-Life Parenthood.*

————. *Because I Said So: 33 Mothers Write About Children, Sex, Men, Aging, Faith, Race & Themselves.*

Newman, Catherine. *Waiting for Birdy: A Year of Frantic Tedium, Neurotic Angst, and the Wild Magic of Growing a Family.*

Peskowitz, Miriam. *The Truth Behind the Mommy Wars.*

Reid, Theresa. *Two Little Girls: A Memoir of Adoption.*

Rough, Bonnie J. *Carrier: Untangling the Danger in my DNA.*

St. Vincent Vogl, Kate. *Lost and Found: A Memoir of Mothers.*

Slater, Lauren. *Love Works Like This.*

Strong, Shari MacDonald, ed. *The Maternal is Political: Women Writers on the Intersection of Motherhood and Social Change.*

Wolfson, Penny. *Moonrise: One Family, Genetic Identity, and Muscular Dystrophy.*

Mother Poets

Fennelly, Beth Ann. *Tender Hooks.*

Garrison, Deborah. *The Second Child.*

Howe, Marie. *The Kingdom of Ordinary Time.*

Keenan, Deborah. *Willow Room, Green Door: New and Selected Poems.*

Olds, Sharon. *Satan Says.*

————. *The Dead and the Living.*

————. *Gold Cell.*

————. *The Unswept Room.*

Literary Journals and Magazines
Brain, Child: The Magazine for Thinking Mothers
Brevity: A Journal of Concise Literary Nonfiction
Errant Parent
Hip Mama
Literary Mama

ADDITIONAL WRITING PROMPTS

In each these exercises, be as specific as possible and try to ground your writing in concrete, sensory details.

What did you think about parenthood and parenting before you became a mother? What did you imagine motherhood would be like? Are there one or two images that stick out in your mind? How is the reality different from or similar to this dream? Focus, if you can, on specific images.

What has been the hardest part of being a mother? Think in terms of moments, days, weeks when things were especially challenging.

What has been one of the most rewarding aspects of being a mother? What are some of the joyful moments of mothering that you didn't expect?

In what ways have you changed (or not changed) since becoming a mother? Make a list and pick one to expand on.

Think back to before you were a mother. Is there something you said or thought that you now wish you could revise? If you could step back in time, what would you tell your younger, less experienced self?

What kind of world do you want your children and grandchildren to live in? Be as specific as possible. Does this world exist?

Make a list of things you didn't expect to feel or say as a mother. Take a few minutes to expand on each of the things on your list. If one of these things leads you somewhere else, go with it.

Think of a moment or situation with your child or children about which you feel guilty. Describe it in as much detail as possible. Try to avoid words like *sad* and *upset*. Ground the scene in concrete details.

Is there anything about being a mother that you are afraid to admit or discuss? What is it? Why does this frighten you?

Begin with "I remember..." and create a list of small memories or moments from the time your child was an infant, a toddler, a child, or a teenager. Do not stop or censor yourself. Focus on sensory details. Think in terms of smell, sound, taste, touch, and sight.

Mother love: What does this term mean to you? What is mother love? Let your mind wander until you focus in on scenes and moments that feel like what you would call "mother love."

Make a list of rituals you had or have with your children, your parents, and your grandparents. What are the smells, sounds, tastes you associate with these rituals? Use as many details as you can to describe one of these rituals.

Find a photo of your family (either your family of origin or your own family). Describe the details of the photograph. Then, try to write what's not in the photo. When was it taken? Who took it? What was going on in your lives when the photo was taken? If you don't know, try "perhapsing."

Remember: Don't pick up your pen—just keep moving it across the paper—and don't worry about grammar or spelling. You don't need to show these first drafts to anyone.

FINDING AN AGENT—RESOURCES & TIPS

Searching for an agent
www.agentquery.com
Ask Allison: www.allisonwinnscotch.blogspot.com
Writer's Digest *Guide to Literary Agents*
Writing conferences
Similar books, acknowledgment pages

Writing a query letter
Why are you approaching this agent?
Paragraph overview of memoir
Description of market
Offer to send proposal or first chapters
Thank agent for time and consideration

Questions to consider when speaking with an interested agent
How will you pitch this book to editors?
Can you describe the process of pitching this book? How many editors will you send my manuscript to?
Please describe how you view the author–agent relationship.
Would you consider yourself an editorial agent?
What kinds of contacts do you have with magazines and newspapers? If I send you an article or essay, will you help me place it?

CONTRIBUTORS

CECELIE S. BERRY's essays have been published in the *New York Times*, the *Washington Post*, *Newsweek*, *O: The Oprah Magazine*, and Salon.com. Her commentary has been broadcast on NPR's *Morning Edition* and on WNYC. She is the author of the anthology *Rise Up Singing: Black Women Writers on Motherhood* (Doubleday 2004), which received an American Book Award. She is currently working on a screenplay.

MARILYN BOUSQUIN received her MFA in creative nonfiction from Ashland University in 2011. She has worked as a children's book reviewer, an educational writer, an editor, and a reader for *River Teeth*. She is currently writing a memoir that explores the connections between letters her devoutly Catholic grandmother wrote during WWII and her own experiences of faith and motherhood.

ANNE GREENWOOD BROWN is an attorney, married with three tween and teen children. She writes essays, short stories, and MG/YA fiction. The first book in her YA series about murderous mermaids on Lake Superior will be published by Random House Children's Books/ Delacorte Press in summer 2012. She is a guest blogger on *Writer Unboxed*, and you can find her at http://annegreenwoodbrown.com.

JILL CHRISTMAN's memoir, *Darkroom: A Family Exposure*, won the AWP Award Series in Creative Nonfiction in 2001; University of Georgia Press reissued *Darkroom* in paperback in fall 2011. She teaches creative nonfiction in Ashland University's low-residency MFA program and at Ball State University in Muncie, Indiana, where she lives with her husband, writer Mark Neely, and their two children. Find more essays and news at www.jillchristman.com.

JUDITH ORTIZ COFER is the award-winning author of 14 books of poetry and prose, including the recent *Lessons from a Writer's Life: Readings and Resources for Teachers and Students* (2011) and *If I Could Fly*, a novel (2011). She is currently the Regents' and Franklin Professor of English and Creative Writing at the University of Georgia. She lives in Athens, Georgia, and Louisville, Georgia, with her husband, John Cofer, a fellow educator.

LINDA LEE CROSFIELD's poetry has been published in *Room*, *Horsefly*, *The New Orphic Review*, *The Minnesota Review*, *Labor*, *The Antigonish Review*, and in several chapbooks and anthologies. She blogs at www.purplemountainpoems.blogspot.com and is working on her first poetry manuscript. She lives, writes, and makes books in Ootischenia (which means "valley of consolation" in Russian), at the confluence of the Columbia and Kootenay Rivers in Southeast British Columbia.

LUCINDA CUMMINGS is a psychologist and writer who lives in Minneapolis. She has published essays in *mamazine* and *Mom Writers Literary Magazine*. She is working on a book-length memoir.

CHITRA DIVAKARUNI, an award-winning and internationally best-selling writer and poet, is the author of 15 books, including the short story collection *Arranged Marriage*, which won an American Book Award, and the novels *Sister of My Heart*, *The Mistress of Spices*, *Queen of Dreams*, and *The Palace of Illusions*. She is the Betty and Gene McDavid Professor of Creative Writing at the University of Houston.

ONA GRITZ is an award-winning poet, columnist, and the author of two children's books. Her poetry chapbook, *Left Standing*, was published by Finishing Line Press in 2005. Ona's essays have been published in numerous anthologies and journals, most recently *Utne Reader*, *More* magazine, and *The Bellingham Review*. Her monthly column on mothering and disability can be found online at www.literarymama.com. She has received eight Pushcart nominations for her work.

SUSAN ITO is editor of the literary anthology *A Ghost At Heart's Edge: Stories & Poems of Adoption* (North Atlantic Books). She has written a column for and is creative nonfiction editor at the online literary journal *Literary Mama*. Her work has appeared in *Growing Up Asian American, Choice, Making More Waves*, and elsewhere.

BETH KEPHART is the award-winning author of memoirs, poetry, history, fable, and novels for young adults. Her 13th book, *You Are My Only* (Egmont USA) was released in October 2011, and she is at work on an adult novel and a new memoir. Kephart is a strategic partner in an award-winning boutique communications firm, teaches memoir at the University of Pennsylvania, and maintains a popular blog, www.beth-kephart.blogspot.com.

SARA MARTIN lives in Minneapolis with her husband, two young sons, and a very patient dog. Both boys joined her family through adoption. Sara tries to squeeze in some writing when she's not spending time with her family, working as a public defender, or training for triathlons.

CATHERINE NEWMAN is the author of the award-winning memoir *Waiting for Birdy* and writes regularly for many magazines, including *FamilyFun, O: The Oprah Magazine, Real Simple, Brain, Child,* and *Whole Living*. She writes about cooking and parenting on her blog at www.benandbirdy.blogspot.com. Her work has been published in numerous anthologies.

LISA KAHN SCHNELL, known by two charming girls as Big Bad Green Mommy, writes for children and adults, leads a summer nature camp, and dances. Her twisty path has led her to a hilltop in Pennsylvania, where she and her family share their home with a Ghanaian cat, six chickens, and the occasional snapping turtle.

SUE WILLIAM SILVERMAN's memoir *Love Sick: One Woman's Journey through Sexual Addiction* is also a Lifetime television movie. Her first memoir, *Because I Remember Terror, Father, I Remember You*, won the AWP award in creative nonfiction, while her craft book, *Fearless Confessions: A Writers Guide to Memoir*, was awarded Honorable Mention in *ForeWord Review's* book-of-the-year award in the category of Writing. She teaches writing at the Vermont College of Fine Arts. Please visit www.suewilliamsilverman.com.

NICOLE COLLINS STARSINIC's poems have appeared in *Literary Mama* and in the Sacramento Poetry Center's *PoetryNow*. She lives in Northern California with her family. She is currently in school for her master's in Counseling and looks forward to the day she can practice as a Marriage and Family Therapist.

ERIN WHITE's work has appeared in *Creative Nonfiction, Literary Mama*, and elsewhere. She lives in western Massachusetts with her family.

ALEXIS WOLFE lives in Ascot, UK, with her husband, Neil, and children, Jacob and Reuben. Participating in Kate's online writing course for mothers encouraged her to start writing.

CREDITS AND COPYRIGHT NOTICES

Excerpts from *Small Continents*, by Kate Hopper, reprinted with permission of the author. Copyright © 2012 by Kate Hopper.

"Bee Sting," by Susan Ito, copyright © 2012 by Susan Ito. Reprinted with permission of the author.

"Samuel," by Susan Ito, originally appeared in *It's a Boy: Women Writers on Raising Sons,* edited by Andrea J. Buchanan, published by Seal Press. Copyright © 2005 by Susan Ito. Reprinted with permission of the author.

Excerpt from *Love You To Pieces: Creative Writers on Raising a Child with Special Needs,* by Suzanne Kamata, copyright © 2008 by Suzanne Kamata. Reprinted with permission of Beacon Press.

"The Line Is White and It Is Narrow," by Beth Kephart, originally appeared in *Mothers Who Think: Tales of Real-Life Parenthood,* edited by Camille Peri and Kate Moses, published by Washington Square Press. Copyright © 1999 by Beth Kephart. Reprinted with permission of the author.

Excerpt from *A Slant of Sun: One Child's Courage,* by Beth Kephart, copyright © 1998 by Beth Kephart. Reprinted with permission of W.W. Norton and Company, Inc.

" 'Perhapsing': The Use of Speculation in Creative Nonfiction," by Lisa Knopp, originally appeared in *Brevity,* Issue 29. Copyright © 2009 by Lisa Knopp. Reprinted with permission of the author.

Excerpt from *Operating Instructions: A Journal of My Son's First Year,* by Anne Lamott, copyright © 1993 by Anne Lamott. Used by permission of Random House and The Wylie Agency LLC.

Excerpt from Alexis Wolfe's memoir-in-progress copyright © 2010 by Alexis Wolfe. Reprinted with permission of the author.

Excerpts from interviews with Hope Edelman, Vicki Forman, Deborah Garrison, Debra Gwartney, Sonya Huber, Beth Kephart, and Julie Schumacher originally appeared on Kate Hopper's personal blog, www.motherhoodandwords.com, or in personal correspondence with the authors. Reprinted with permission of the authors.

Comments by Kate's students reprinted with their permission.

WORKS CITED

Bazelon, Emily. "Is This Tantrum on the Record?: The ground rules for writing about your kids." *Slate*, June 5, 2008 http://www.slate. com/id/2192374/.

Berry, Cecelie. "Was He Black or White?" *Because I Said So: 33 Mothers Write About Children, Sex, Men, Aging, Faith, Race, & Themselves.* Kate Moses and Camille Peri, eds. New York: HarperCollins, 2005.

Brown, Anne Greenwood. "Insights." *Literary Mama.* April 25, 2010. http://www.literarymama.com/creativenonfiction/archives/2010/ 04/insights.html.

Christman, Jill. "The Allergy Diaries." *Harpur Palate* vol. 6.2, Winter 2007: 100–121.

— —. "Three Takes on a Jump." *Mississippi Review.* Special Summer 2006 Issue: Partly True (2,000 words).

Cofer, Judith Ortiz. "Five A.M.: Writing as Ritual." *The Latin Deli: Prose and Poetry.* Athens: University of Georgia Press, 1993.

Crosfield, Linda Lee. "Packing the Car." *Literary Mama.* January 5, 2005. http://www.literarymama.com/poetry/archives/2005/01/ packing-the-car.html.

Cummings, Lucinda. "My Mother Is Missing." *mamazine* Sept. 2, 2007. http://www.mamazine.com/Pages/feature99.html.

DiCamillo, Kate. Reading Rockets interview with Kate DiCamillo. http://www.readingrockets.org/books/interviews/dicamillo/.

Dillard, Annie. "To Fashion a Text." *The Fourth Genre: Contemporary Writers of/on Creative Nonfiction*, 2nd ed. Robert Root and Michael Steinberg, eds. New York: Longman, 2002.

Divakaruni, Chitra. "Common Scents: The Smell of Childhood Never Fades." *Salon* 26 June 1997. http://www1.salon.com/june97/mothers/chitra970626.html

Edelman, Hope. E-mail interview with Kate Hopper. Jan. 25, 2010.

Forman, Vicki. E-mail interview with Kate Hopper. June 1, 2011.

Frank, Anne. *The Diary of a Young Girl.* New York: Bantam, 1993.

Garrison, Deborah. Phone interview with Kate Hopper. June 20, 2007.

Gerard, Philip. "The Fact Behind the Facts." *Brevity* 27 (May 2008). http://www.creativenonfiction.org/brevity/craft/craft_gerard_26.html.

Goldberg, Natalie. *Writing Down the Bones: Freeing the Writer Within.* Boston: Shambhala, 1986.

Gornick, Vivian. *The Situation and the Story: The Art of Personal Narrative.* New York: Farrar, Straus and Giroux, 2001.

Gritz, Ona. "This." *Literary Mama,* Nov. 26, 2006. http://www.literarymama.com/poetry/archives/2006/11/this.html.

Gwartney, Debra. E-mail interview with Kate Hopper. July 13, 2010.

Hampl, Patricia. "Memory and Imagination." *I Could Tell You Stories: Sojourns in the Land of Memory.* New York: W.W. Norton & Co., 1999.

Hirsch, Kathleen, and Katrina Kenison. *Mothers: Twenty Stories of Contemporary Motherhood.* New York: North Point Press, 1996.

Hopper, Kate. "It's Not a Hobby: Writing and the Value of Non-paid Work." *Women Writing on Family: Tips on Writing, Teaching, and Publishing.* Colleen S. Harris and Carol Smallwood, eds. Toronto: Key Publishing House, Inc., 2012.

Huber, Sonya. E-mail interview with Kate Hopper. January 11, 2011.

Ito, Susan. "Samuel." *It's a Boy: Women Writers on Raising Sons.* Andrea Buchanan, ed. Berkeley: Seal Press, 2005.

Kamata, Suzanne. *Love You To Pieces: Creative Writers on Raising a Child with Special Needs.* Boston: Beacon Press, 2008.

Kephart, Beth. *A Slant of Sun: One Child's Courage.* New York: W.W. Norton & Co., 1998.

———. E-mail correspondence with Kate Hopper. April 5, 2009.

———. "The Line is White, and It Is Narrow." *Mothers Who Think: Tales of Real-Life Parenthood.* Kate Moses and Camille Peri, eds. New York: Washington Square Books, 1999.

Knopp, Lisa. "'Perhapsing': The Use of Speculation in Creative Nonfiction." *Brevity* 29 (Winter 2009) http://www.creativenonfiction. org/brevity/craft/craft_knopp1_09.htm.

Lamott, Anne. *Bird by Bird: Some Instructions on Writing and Life.* New York: Pantheon Books, 1994.

———. *Operating Instructions: A Journal of My Son's First Year.* New York: Pantheon Books, 1993.

Lott, Bret. "Toward a Definition of Creative Nonfiction." *The Fourth Genre: Contemporary Writers of/on Creative Nonfiction,* 2nd ed. Robert Root and Michael Steinberg, eds. New York: Longman, 2002.

Martin, Sara. "Music in His Genes." *Adoptive Families* (2007). http:// www.adoptivefamilies.com/articles.php?aid=1534.

Newman, Catherine. "Pretty Baby." *It's a Boy: Women Writers on Raising Sons.* Andrea Buchanan, ed. Berkeley: Seal Press, 2005.

Pomeroy, Carrie. "Challenges, Discoveries and Surprises of Writing Creative Nonfiction about My Mother." Association of Writers and Writing Programs Annual Conference. Chicago, Feb. 14, 2009.

Rico, Gabriel. *Writing the Natural Way,* 15th Anniversary Expanded Edition. New York: Tarcher/Putnam, 2000.

Schnell, Lisa Kahn. "Circling." *Brevity* 22 (Fall 2006). http://www. creativenonfiction.org/brevity/past%20issues/brev22/schnell_ circling.htm.

Schumacher, Julie. E-mail interview with Kate Hopper. March 23, 2009.

Silverman, Sue William. *Fearless Confessions: A Writer's Guide to Memoir.* Athens: University of Georgia Press, 2009.

Starsinic, Nicole Collins. "How the story begins." *Literary Mama* 5, Dec. 2010. http://www.literarymama.com/poetry/archives/2010/12/how-the-story-begins.html.

White, Erin. "Book Bind." *Literary Mama* 3, Oct. 2010. http://www.literarymama.com/columns/henhouse/archives/2010/book_bind.html.

Wolfson, Penny. "Voice Lessons." *Sarah Lawrence College Magazine* (Spring 2003). http://www.slc.edu/magazine/who-are-you/Voice_Lessons.php.

Zinsser, William. *On Writing Well: The Classic Guide to Writing Nonfiction,* 6th ed. New York: HarperPerennial, 1998.

ACKNOWLEDGMENTS

I am incredibly grateful to the Loft Literary Center, who welcomed me into their community and gave my class for mother writers a home. Your work in the literary community can't be measured. Thank you to all my students who have shared their stories and lives with me. You have made me not only a better writer and teacher, but a better mother and person. Your words have incredible power. Don't forget it.

Thank you to my amazing agent, Amy Burkhardt, for her keen editorial eye and for believing in me and this book. I am so lucky to work with you, and I owe you a dinner if we're ever in the same city. Thank you to the whole team at Viva Editions and Cleis Press, especially Felice Newman and Brenda Knight for seeing the value in this book, and Nancy Fish, for helping me get it out into the world. Thank you also to Mark Rhynsburger for his careful editing.

To the many writers and poets who have let me use their words in this book and in my classes: I couldn't have written this without your stories and poems, which amaze and inspire me. I am grateful for your writing and your generosity of spirit.

I would not be the teacher I am if it were not for the wonderful writing teachers with whom I've had the honor to work. Thank you especially to Charles Baxter, Barrie Jean Borich, Patricia Hampl, and Julie Schumacher. I am grateful for what you taught me about craft, but also for what you showed me about being a warm and generous teacher.

Thank you to all the people who helped me write this book: To Susan Ito and Violeta Garcia Mendoza for helping me launch my class for mother writers online, an act that turned out to be the first seeds of this book; to Jeff Shotts for his feedback on an early draft of my book proposal; to Caroline Grant and Vicki Forman, for their friendship and early support. To Kay Krhin, for her unwavering support and spectacular brainstorming. To Suzanne Kamata, Jennifer Niesslein, Sharon Kraus and Ginny Kaczmarek for their timely suggestions.

I am forever grateful to my writing group, Rob McGinley Myers and Rhena Tantisunthorn Refsland, for their generous and insightful feedback. I owe you many rounds of drinks. And I'm humbled by the help with permissions that I received from the following people: Michele Burwell, Betty Knudson, Kay Krhin, Sara Martin, Rob McGinley Myers, Rhena Tantisunthorn Refsland, Patty Born Selly, and Kara Thom.

So many friends have supported me as I wrote this book. Thank you especially to Teri Blair, Diane Brown, Jill Christman, Kate Freeborn, Claire Haiman, Jess Hopeman, Rachel Hopper and Josh Williams, Sara Hopper and Shawn Sullivan, Laura and Mike LaFave, Kristine Miller, Paige Parranto, Bonnie J. Rough, Emily Sellergren, and Kara Douglass Thom.

I couldn't have written a word of this book without my family. Thank you to my dad, David Hopper, and to my mom and step-dad, Nancy and Karl Olson. I am deeply grateful for your constant support, your incredible generosity, and the childcare you are always willing to provide so I can have an extra hour—or four—to write. To my sisters, Rachel Hopper and Sara Hopper, for their pep talks and cackling laughter. To my grandpa, Spencer Nelson, who died at age 102 before this book was published: Thank you for showing me how to live a full life. Your love and belief in me live on.

Finally: Thank you to Donny—my best friend, my love, and my greatest supporter—and to my girls, Stella and Zoë, who have made my life what it is. I'm grateful, and I love you.

ABOUT THE AUTHOR

KATE HOPPER TEACHES WRITING ONLINE AND AT The Loft Literary Center in Minneapolis, where she lives with her husband and two daughters. Kate holds an MFA in creative writing from the University of Minnesota and has been the recipient of a Fulbright Scholarship, a Minnesota State Arts Board Grant, and a Sustainable Arts Grant. Her writing has appeared in a number of journals, including *Brevity*, *Literary Mama*, and *The New York Times* online. She is an editor at *Literary Mama*. For more information about Kate's writing and classes, visit www.katehopper.com.

Photograph by Nancy Reins.

INDEX

❧❧

TO OUR READERS

Viva Editions publishes books that inform, enlighten, and entertain. We do our best to bring you, the reader, quality books that celebrate life, inspire the mind, revive the spirit, and enhance lives all around. Our authors are practical visionaries: people who offer deep wisdom in a hopeful and helpful manner. Viva was launched with an attitude of growth and we want to spread our joy and offer our support and advice where we can to help you live the Viva way: vivaciously!

We're grateful for all our readers and want to keep bringing you books for inspired living. We invite you to write to us with your comments and suggestions, and what you'd like to see more of. You can also sign up for our online newsletter to learn about new titles, author events, and special offers.

Viva Editions
2246 Sixth St.
Berkeley, CA 94710
www.vivaeditions.com
(800) 780-2279
Follow us on Twitter @vivaeditions
Friend/fan us on Facebook